WOMEN'S MOVEMENTS

WOMEN'S MOVEMENTS

By

Dr. B. Suguna

Dept. of Women's Studies
Sri Padmavati Mahila Visvavidyalayam
Tirupati – 517 502
Andhra Pradesh

DISCOVERY PUBLISHING HOUSE PVT. LTD.
NEW DELHI-110 002

Published by:

DISCOVERY PUBLISHING HOUSE PVT. LTD.
4383/4B, Ansari Road, Darya Ganj
New Delhi-110 002 (India)
Phone : +91-11-23279245; 23253475; 43596065
E-mail : discoverybooksindia@gmail.com
discoverypublishinghouse@gmail.com
namitwasan9@gmail.com
web : www.discoverypublishinggroup.com

***First Edition:* 2009**
***Reprinted:* 2025**

ISBN: 978-81-8356-425-0

Women's Movements

Printed at:
Infinity Imaging Systems
Delhi (India)

Preface

Women's Movement is the organised effort to achieve a common goal of equality and liberation of women and it presupposes sensitiveness to crucial issues affecting the life of women. Women played a very significant role in the history of the Freedom Movement in India. In the 19th and 20th Centuries, several efforts were made by the social and political reformers like Kandukuri Veeresalingam Pantulu, Eswara Chandra Vidya Sagar, Raja Ram Mohan Roy, Swami Dayananda Saraswati, Keshab Chandra Sen, Phoole, Kante, Mahadev Govind Ranade, Swami Vivekananda, Venkata Ratnam Naidu, Annie Besant, Mahatma Gandhiji and others to uplift women, educate them and train them so that they would imbibe the ideas of Nationalism, Patriotism, Liberty, Democracy etc. They actively advocated Women's Education, Abolition of Sati, Child Marriages, Widow Remarriages and other social reforms.

The last three decades have been marked by the growth and development of the women's movement in India. New issues have been raised, new methods are used for bringing awareness among women and different structures are appearing to mobilise women's voice, feelings and their needs. In fact International Women's Decade (1976-1985) provided a leverage to women's movement in India. In the pre-independence period, the women's movement was very much a part of the nationalist movement. The liberal approach to women's issues and overall middle-class urban leadership mark out as significant features of the first phase of women's movement. With independence, when the constitutional equality was guaranteed and the Central Social Welfare Board (1953) evolved grant-in-aid programmes for women's organisations, a period of acquiescence began.

During the sixties, though specific women's issues did not surface prominently, yet women were mobilised in large numbers and they joined the general struggles of the rural poor, tribals, industrial working-class and other mass movements. Participation of women in Chipko Movement, Telangana Movement, Anti-arrack Movement, Anti-rape Movement and Anti-price Rise Movement provided a backdrop for the ensuing struggles on women's issues.

In this context Prof. B. Suguna's book on Women's Movement is very much relevant to the present day situation. This book is an indepth study of women's movements in pre- and post-Independence period. The author has explained elaborately the role and participation of women, women's organizations, Women's associations, in various movements for the upliftment of women. The role of social reformers for the advancement of women is also clearly explained. The book will be highly useful to the students and research scholars of social sciences especially Women's Studies, Sociology, Social Work, Political Science and also the students specialising in Human Development, NGO's and other functionaries dealing with women. I wish the author would bring about many more studies relevant to present day issues of women.

Prof. G. Sarojamma
Vice-Chancellor
S.P.Mahila Visvavidyalayam
TIRUPATI

Contents

Concept, Definition, Basic Elements and Classification of Women's Movements

Women's movements are organised efforts made by women's association to bring about equality and freedom for women. All movements in which women participate are not women's movements. Those movements which are guided by an ideology of fighting the sexual division of labour and patriarchy and which act against specific issues of oppression against women in an uncompromising way are also women's movements. Women's movements can be broadly categorised into movements for liberation and movements for equality. The concept of patriarchy is central to the liberation movement. Some believe that this is to be biological and rooted in the reproductive function, whereas others consider it to have originated socially. The liberationists wish to free women from the oppression of patriarchal control and sex-stereotypes arising from it. Movements for equality emphasise equality of women in education, occupation, legal rights and other areas of family and social life.

Basic Elements of Women's Movements

A study of the components of different Women's Movements is necessary before going into their diversities.

M.S.A. Rao (1978) defines social movements as "an organised effort on the part of a section of population, involving collective mobilisation based on an ideology to bring about change in the social system". In view of the above definition, women's movements can be considered as organised efforts by women's associations, involving collective mobilisation based on an ideology to bring about equality and freedom for women. Thus the basic elements of women's movements can be identified as:

- Collective mobilisation
- Presence of an ideology
- Orientation towards change

Collective Mobilisation

A mass base is indispensable to any movement. Affected masses have to be collectively mobilised into action for change. Creating awareness through education and conscientisation are essential for mobilising the affected masses. Action strategies involve peaceful methods of education, discussions, write ups etc. To move agitational and confrontational tactics for social and legal changes. Agitations form operational parts of movements. But movement is much more than a sum of agitations. Movements have larger perspective and goals to be reached through various techniques including agitation.

Presence of an Ideology

Sociologists agree on the fact that ideology plays a very important role in a movement. In fact ideology forms the basis of any movement. At the base of women's movements is the feminist ideology of women as an oppressed section in struggle against their oppressors.

Gail Omvedt (1986) very lucidly distinguishes between three shades of feminism. "Liberal Feminism" aims at bringing about equality between the sexes, within the framework of existing system. "Radical Feminism" aims at revolutionary changes in all but sees sexual oppression as primary. "Socialist Feminism" attempts to analyse the oppression of women as linked with other forms of oppression and seeks to unite the fight for socialism with that for women's liberation.

Orientation Towards Change

Gusfield (1979) emphasises that social movements are directed towards demand for change in the social order. Nadkarni (1987) affirms that social movements intend to alter the existing social order or power structure at least at the regional level where it takes place. We have women's associations working as pressure groups at various levels. These groups agitate to bring about changes at their own regional level. They also try to establish linkages and work together to bring about changes at the national level. The changes which are aspired by these movements are on the lines of predetermined goals based on the ideology or broad perspectives adopted by the movement.

Classification of Women's Movements

Gail Omvedt (1976) has classified women's movements into four types. They are:

- Movements in which women participate;
- Movement of women for any cause;
- Movements for bringing about reforms for benefitting women;
- Women's liberation movements.

Movements Where Women Participate

Men and women participate in movements such as working class and peasant movements, anti-price rise and other popular movements. Their thrust is against various forms of oppression, which also oppress women. However, they do not focus on oppression due to sexual differentiation and hence they are not women's movements. The organisers of these movements may conceed to some of the special needs of the women in return for their participation in the common goal but once the movement is over, they try to put the women back in their place.

Omvedt feels that although these cannot be equated with full-fledged movements. They play an important role in giving women strength and self-confidence in fighting against their own oppression and also feel the experience of participating openly for a common cause.

Movement of Women

There may be movements on general issues such as price-rise or slum improvement where women are the only participants. But the sole participation of women alone does not make them women's movements. In fact such movements may confirm the gender division of labour where men fight for wage rise and women against price-rise without ever challenging the male-dominated family and social structure. Omvedt rightly says that these movements play a progressive role. Their importance lies in the fact that they give women participants a chance to experience their own collective strength.

Women's Reform Movements

In the pre-independent era there was a spurt of movements on education and voting rights for women, abolition of Sati etc. Although the issues were apparently concerned with women, Omvedt refuses to recognise them as women's movements. The reason for this is that these movements did not challenge the fundamental structures of oppression either in the family or in the society. They were not directly concerned with giving more rights or power to the women, but more concerned with modernising or upgrading the society in ways seen as necessary to maintain traditional values.

Women's Liberation Movements

Movements which are broadly guided by an ideology of fighting the sexual division of labour and patriarchy and which act against specific issue of oppression in an uncompromising way that moves in the direction of liberation can be called women's movements.

Specific issues of Sati or Women's education can be understood and fought against as a part of a broader patriarchal system of oppression. Women's movement does not see women's issues as subordinate to the social goals but keeps them in the focus and then perceives their connection with other social goals.

2

Social Reform Movement and National Movement

Women had played a very significant role in the history of the freedom movement in India. Many believe that the movement would not have been successful but for the participation of women. It is really surprising that women could take such a lead in the movement when it was often believed that they occupied a subservient position in society. It may appear paradoxical but it is true. In the nineteenth and twentieth centuries, several efforts were made by the social and political reformers to uplift women, educate them and train them so that they would imbibe the ideas of nationalism, patriotism, liberty, democracy etc. We come across individuals like Kandukuri Veeresalingam Pantulu, Raghupathi Venkatarathnam Naidu and others and institutions like Brahma Samaj, Women's Indian Association and other associations which occupy foremost place in the emancipation of women. Social freedom is interlinked with political freedom. For the progress of a nation both are a must. Hence, social reform movement and the freedom movement are the two inseparable movements for political liberation, each complementing the other and ultimately ushering in a new political and social order by 1947 in our country. The history of these two movements run over a hundred years.

Strictly speaking, there had been no feminist movement in India, similar to any of those that originated in the West. Although in India the movement had started all of a sudden the participation of women drawn from all classes and its unimagined numbers on the political scene was doubtlessly startling. Raja Rammohan Roy began the movement for the amelioration of women in Indian society and Gandhiji had taken it to its peak. Besides these two giant leaders, there were a number of social reformers both men and women, who were responsible for bringing about a number of social reforms. India was blessed with a galaxy of leaders like Dr. Annie Besant, Mahatma Gandhiji etc. who were staunch believers of women's emancipation. They made the utmost effort to reform women so as to enable them to participate actively in the freedom movement. There were men who, while struggling for political freedom wanted their women to help them in realising women's emancipation. For them as followers of Gandhiji, improvement of women's status became a pre-requisite for political freedom. So, women's movement and political movement came to be intertwined.

Women's movements in India were born out of the same historical circumstances and social milieu as several 19th century social roform movements were born out of. Liberal ideology, which provoked a new thinking about various social institutions and practices also set the Western educated Indians to think about the position and plight of Indian women whose condition was pitiable. Thus the women's movement originated in the historical context of socio-cultural awakening of the 19th century. The women's movement whose origin can be traced to the 19th century has been growing from strength to strength with its focus on issues shifting from one to another as also with its ideological and social content changing from time to time and continued into present times. The movement in its entirety can be divided into the following three distinct phases:

- Social reform movements and social reform legislations in the 19th century;
- National Movement;
- Women's movements after post independence period.

Patriarchy, caste system and several other social and religious ideas and practices which have originated in the ancient Indian social milieu continue to dominate the thinking about the social status and position of Indian women.

For a proper understanding of the social reform movements for the development of women in India, it is necessary to examine the historical background of women that necessitated the social reforms.

Traditional medical and quasi-medical concerns center on the disabilities and weaknesses among men, impotence being a major obsession. In common belief, it is the sexual and biological difference, which is stressed as the basis for social differences. But often this is a rationalisation for quite other factors such as inheritance and property rights and family structure which is the fundamental concern. The symbol of the woman in Indian culture has been a curious intermeshing of low legal status, ritual contempt, sophisticated sexual partnership and deification. The role, status and position of women has been far from static, ranging from what is thought to have been a position of considerable authority and freedom to one of equally considerable subservience.

Status of Women in India—An Historical Overview

Within the Indian sub-continent there have been infinite variations on the status of women diverging according to cultural milieu, family structure, class, caste, property rights and morals. Even the ancient erotic manuals of India have digressed at length on the capabilities and idiosyncrasies of Indian women whereas the male remains comparatively uniform perhaps for the reason that these texts were written largely for the edification and education of the male. The literature on erotica stresses the variations in female types particularly the characteristics of women coming from different parts of the sub-continent.

Traditional medical and quasi-medical concerns on the other hand center on the disabilities and weaknesses among men, impotence being a major obsession. In common belief, it is the sexual and biological difference, which is stressed as the basis for social differences. But often this is a rationalisation for quite other factors such as inheritance and property rights and family structure which is the fundamental concern. The symbol of the woman in Indian culture has been a curious intermeshing of low legal status, ritual contempt, sophisticated sexual partnership and deification. The role, status and position of women has been far from static, ranging from what is thought to have been a position of considerable authority and freedom to one of equally considerable subservience.

Some point to the increasing participation of women in public life and to the changes introduced in their legal status. Others maintain that the position of women has changed very little and that Indian society continues by and large to a male-dominated society.

Social and Economic Levels: Historical Factors

From vedic times, women enjoyed a great deal of freedom. India has perhaps the longest record of famous women in mythology and history. History too has shown that women have been able to display outstanding capacities as administrators, states women and warriors. The poet-Queen Meera Bai of the 15th century; Nurjahan, who guided the policy of Jahangir the Mughal Emperor for more than a decade; Muntaz Begum whose beauty inspired the love of Shah Jahan of Mughal Emperor and who has been immortalised in the Taj Mahal at Agra; Ahalya Bai the warrior queen and Rani Lakshmi Bai of Jhansi, known as the Indian Joan of Arc fighting and dying for the freedom of her kingdom against the British. These and many other distinguished leaders in different spheres of religion, philosophy and statesmanship and in qualities of wisdom and learning, courage and imagination did much for social justice of our country, such women, part of the cultural history of India, who have gone into the legend and folk stories provide evidence of the fact that in the early history of India there existed opportunities for education and self-expression until the time of the foreign invasions from the north-west. However in spite of the existence of these exceptional women, there was no system of organised education for women for about eight centuries (1000 to 1800 AD) owing to political and economic unrest and foreign invasions.

Certain social customs such as early marriage, seclusion of women (purdah system), etc. were largely responsible for the disabilities suffered by Indian women during these years. The fear that the unmarried young women were likely to be unprotected when raids were common was perhaps responsible for the early marriage system. It was largely the same fear that made young widows join their deceased husbands in the funeral pyre. The system known as Sati was stopped by law only during the British regime in 1829 and declared a criminal offence. The need for early marriage might have also been responsible for the growth of the cruel dowry system that prevailed for centuries in India and still persists among some social classes. During these dark years, women generally were forbidden to go out unaccompanied beyond the four walls of their houses or courtyards. However among the lower classes, peasant and working women there has always been a greater freedom of movement all over India.

Thus for centuries, the idea that it was almost divinely ordained that women should have inferior status was present in India.

Status of Women in Vedic Period

The position of women was fairly satisfactory at the dawn of civilisation during the Vedic age. The society, as a whole, showed proper concern and respect for women allowing them considerable freedom in the different activities of the social and political life. Ordinarily girls were less welcome than boys but nevertheless girls were educated like boys and had to pass through a period of Brahmacharya. Many of them became distinguished poets.

The marriage of girls used to take place at the age of 16 or 17. By then a large percentage of girls were fairly conversant with religious rituals. Educated girls of this age had an effective voice in the choice of their husbands. Very often there were love marriages which were subsequently blessed by parents. There was no seclusion of women and they used to move about freely in society. In social and religious functions they occupied a prominent position. Women had an absolute equality with men in the eyes of religion. They could perform sacrifices independently on par with men.

Since girls were married at the age of 16 or 17, the period before marriage was utilised for imparting education to them. For 7 to 8 years before marriage they used to learn by heart the Vedic hymns. Women poets themselves were reported to have been composing hymns. Some of them were mentioned in the Rig Veda. Lopamudra, Visvavara, Sikata Nivavari and Ghosha, Apala contributed to the Vedic hymns. We also come across the names of women scholars such as Sulabha Maitreyi, Vadava Prathiteyi and Gargi Vachaknavi who had made contributions to the advance of education. The reported searching cross examination of Yajnavalkya by Gargi shows her high standard of philosophical discourse. Atreyi was another woman student of Vedanta who had studied under the sages Valmiki and Agastya.

Besides studying Vedas many of them specialised in purvamimansa which discussed the diverse problems connected with Vedic sacrifices. Leelavathi assisted her father Bhaskaracharya who was an eminent mathematician. Khana was a great astronomer of that time. When the reaction against the Vedic sacrificial religion gave a stimulus to philosophical speculations at about 800 BC, women, scholars took keen interest in them. One of them happened to be Maitreyi, wife of Yajnavalkya. The tradition of women scholars was mentioned in the puranas. The Bhagavata, for instance refers to two daughters of Dakshayana as experts in theology and philosophy.

In ordinary Kshatriya families women used to receive military training. Women guards of kings belonged to this class.

South Indian inscriptions of the medieval period reveal the existence of many Kshatriya women defending their homes in times of danger.

Military training to women continued in the Maratha royal families. For example, Tarabai, the founder of Kolhapur State, used to lead her troops in person. Princess Kamalabai Scindia, the sister of the present Maharaja of Gwalior and Laxmibai of Jhansi were well known for their remarkable bravery.

Music, dancing and painting were encouraged in the case of girls. Spinning and weaving were encouraged. Kautilya's Arthasastra laid down that the State should provide special facilities to women to enable them to earn a living by spinning and weaving cotton and woolen yarn.

Status of Women—The Sutra Period

In the Sutra Period, the position of women is not as equal as in the vedic times. It was the spirit of the time to crave for more male children, because they wanted more men to fight against the aborigines. Males of all ranks were looked upon with preferential treatment. Women were relegated to household duties. This is the result of the Aryan's intense fighting with the natives. Success against the original inhabitants was followed by the capture of their women and to employ them for household duties. Hence the shadow of the ill-treatment of Non-Aryan women casts its evil seeds upon the dignity of the Aryan women. Polygamy automatically entered into the social life of the Aryans. The Aryans were using 'soma' the gift of gods at the vedic sacrifices in which both sexes participated. Soma was a mild and useful beverage in the colder regions and it became powerful intoxicant in the warm climate. Women were incapable of withstanding this powerful intoxication. As men had to fight against the dasyus, they required more strength. They discovered a stronger drink like sura. But women were gradually proved to be incapable of using these intoxicating drinks which went round men and women at the sacrifices. Women were kept away gradually from using these drinks. As the drinks were served at the vedic sacrifices women in course of time, as they were not using the drinks were kept away from the sacrificial ceremonies also. At the sacrificial ceremonies Vedas were recited. As women did not participate in the sacrificial ceremonies, they eventually began to lose touch with the Vedas and finally the study of the Vedas fell into the hands of men who monopolised their study. As the study of the Vedas was the only source of knowledge became the monopoly of men and women were pushed back to domestic duties. Gradually the gulf between men and women widened. As a result women's right to enjoy equal status with men deteriorated.

Perceptions About Women's Status

Badarayana and Jaimini fought at this time for the revival of womanhood on vedic injunctions. They pleaded for equal rights of women. But the times were against them. Women had already been kept out of the vedic sacrifices and from the study of the Vedas. Gautama declared that women had no right to perform sacrifices, nor they had a right to study the Vedas. They were deprived of all the rights to property, inheritance and adoption. He regarded woman as property.

Vasishta and Baudhayana were hard on women. They said that men were their masters and so women should never be independent. Since women did not study the Vedas, they declared that women had no right to participate in the sacrifices. They declared that women should not have the right to property. Since women were regarded as property, marriage by purchase came into existence. Niyoga was disrespected and remarriages were discouraged. An ascetic must remove her hair on the head. Hence it appears to have been originated from this source the custom of disfiguring the Indian widow. During the later stages of this period the wife had gained equal right to property with her husband. Yet the widow was not allowed to inherit the property.

Manu and Katyayana upheld the cause of womanhood. Manu said that a wife should not be abused if she had abandoned a husband who was impotent, insane or suffering from an incurable disease. If the widow's previous marriage was not consummated she should be permitted to remarry. The children born of them had a legal claim to property. He further declared that women could not perform sacrifices, nor could they study the Vedas, he added that "gods dwell where women were honoured". A husband could cast off his wife, but a wife could never do so. He said that a wife, a son and a slave should not have property rights. He said that women should not have independence. In childhood she should be protected by her father, when an adult she should be protected by her husband, and in her old age she should be protected by her sons. He declared that a girl of 8 years should be given away in marriage. At the same time he added that a girl could remain rather unmarried than to be wedded to an unworthy husband. From the above it may be concluded that Manu's code is full of contradictions as regards the status of women.

Yagnavalkya and Parasara tried to improve the status of women. They recognised women's property rights. Any gifts made to her by her relatives were regarded her own. The mother was entitled for a share in the property. Women were allowed to lend and borrow money. Assaults on women were tried and punished. If the husband deserted a wife for no reason, she had a right to claim one third of his property. Narada and Parasara declared that widows could remarry.

Mitakshara declared that as women were generally weak, physically they should be protected by fathers, brothers, husbands and sons. He said that the idea of "Stree Dharma" carried with it the idea of women's capacity to hold property. Jimutavahana and Vignaneswara emphasised more on women's property rights. Vidyaranya also emphasised the right of women to property.

Status of Women in the Medieval Period

In the Medieval times, Padmini the heroine, Ahalya Bai the great administrator enlightened the people with their scholarship. Lakshmi Devi wrote 'Vividachandra'. This period is also known for the works of the great authoress Kalyani sister of Madhavacharya. The Bhakti teaching produced the women 'saints' – Andal, Meera Bai and Lalla.

During the Mughal period, seclusion of women was looked upon as a symbol of respectability among the higher classes. But women in general, especially those belonging to the agricultural and working classes, did not observe purdah. The birth of a female child was unwelcome both in Hindu and Muslim families and the evil of infanticide was prevalent in some sections of society. Even Muslims adopted the system of early marriage and dowry. They were generally polygamous. Akbar, however, ordered that a man of ordinary means should not have more than one wife. Hindus, except those of the ruling and wealthy classes were strictly monogamous. The practice of widow-remarriage except in lower castes disappeared. Women themselves resented remarriage and sati became popular. Although emperor Humayun wanted to prohibit sati, he could not do so. Akbar was also against the practice and adopted rigorous measures to prevent the forcible burning of widows.

Only in rare cases women were given any education except to those belonging to the elite class whose daughters were given opportunities for religious learning and mental discipline. However, despite the many social disabilities, women were happy and contented during the Mughal period. Akbar held the Hindu women in high esteem. In his opinion, they were 'flaming torches of love and fellowship". Jahangir also admired Hindu women for their single-minded devotion and fidelity.

Status of Indian Women in the 19th Century

It was a common belief till tho 19th century that women were fit only for household activites and that their place was in the kitchen. Margaret Cousins, in her book "Indian Womanhood Today", opined that viewing from different dimensions like literacy, individuality, health, social status, freedom of movement and economic independence, the condition of women in the 19th century in general all over India was at its lowest ebb. The "Friend of India" in its issue supported the above view. The need for liberation of women was felt in India in the 19th century as the women underwent considerable sufferings and miseries specially during the 19th century. Girls were not wanted as children and their presence was not welcome. Similar situation existed with some variations in Andhra as well.

Female Infanticide

One of the social evils that women had to face in those days was female infanticide. Birth of a female child was not welcome even by parents and they were exposed to death. According to tradition, son the heir apparent is the only person who is the saviour of the parents. He performs the last rites to his parents without which it is believed that parents have no salvation (cannot go to heaven). Further, the husband and the wife have no right to perform a number of religious ceremonies if they are childless. So if they have no son, it is customary to adopt a boy who would make them eligible for performing many rites. Thus, son is a 'must' in the Hindu family. On the other hand birth of a girl is largely looked down upon even now. Tod writes that Rajputs were often heard to explain "accursed the day when a girl child was born". Even though we do not have categorical evidence of female infanticide in Andhra, birth of a girl child does not receive spontaneous welcome in several families even today.

Child Marriage

The second social evil that persisted in the society was child marriage. Dr. Annie Besant had a great regard for the Hindu custom of marriage and the ideal of this *samskara* – which she said, did not exist anywhere in the world. But this system lost its significance as well as validity because of the introduction of child marriages in India in the later periods of history due to various reasons. So, she said 'there is no ideal of marriage anywhere known which is more exquisitely beautiful than the Hindu ideal but it is trampled in the mud'. Girls were married at very young age i.e. between the ages of one to ten years and sometimes less than a year leaving no opportunity for them to improve their physical or mental health. Early marriages were celebrated because the young girl at the time of marriage could adjust herself to her husband and his relations as well as to the new setup. But one of the abuses of this custom was that the wife lacked the knowledge of a married life and its responsibilities. The life in the new environment became miserable as the mother-in-law and other relations used to torture her. The girl child thus underwent suffering right from her birth, as a female child, as a child wife as a child-mother and very often as a child widow.

This system blocked all the channels of development—physical, mental and even spiritual. It resulted in crushing the individuality of the child wife. Early marriage and early consummation curtailed freedom and joy of girlhood. The practice of child marriage was responsible for the high rate of infant mortality. Fuller observes, "of children born every year, only about half the number reached the age of thirteen years".

Several efforts were made by Raja Rammohan Roy and other social reformers to fight against this social evil. In Andhra Pradesh, social reformers like Kandukuri, Venkatarathnam Naidu and others had dedicated their lives for this cause.

Sati

Sati, though not obligatory was also performed in the state of Andhra Pradesh. The siege of Bobbili by Bussy in 1757 was followed by the self-immolation of women en masse. In Peddapuram, around 1734, the reigning Zamindar Timma died in a fight with Rustum Khan. Timma's mother Rangamma arranged the fire and all women threw themselves into it. Sitamma belonging to the same family also performed Sati in 1760 when her husband died fighting with Ananda Gajapathi of Vijayanagaram. The two wives of Ananda Gajapathi committed Sati when he died at Rajahmundry. This practice prevailed in Nuzvidu family too. When Raja Narasimha Apparao and his successor Sobhanadri Apparao died, their wives preferred sati. Sitamma, wife of Venkatadri Apparao also followed her deceased husband in this way in 1771. When Narasimha Appa Rao died in 1789 his wife was dissuaded from the act of self-immolation by a European officer commanding the station. Vennelakanti Subbarao's journal mentions that he has an eye witness in Guntur when the widow of Tomoo Papaiah practiced Sati in 1822. The instance of a woman Atchayamma who committed Sati was mentioned by Fancis. The Act passed during 1829 was applied to the entire country and might have prevented the recurrence of the event. The elite was also reacting against this practice as is known to us from *Kasiyatra Charitra*. Veeraswamy convinced the local pandits at Gaya that *Moola smritis* do not support Sati and hence it was not an obligation. He did not go beyond to consider the plight of young widows. This account reveals that the practice of Sati was confined to royal and zamindari families. Thus in this state, unlike in Bengal this was not practiced by common people.

This social evil was a great obstacle in the life of women. So, social reformers had taken greatest care to see that this system would completely vanish. Fortunately in Andhra Pradesh when British government forbade Sati, efforts were made to put an end to this practice.

Enforced Widowhood

The child marriage had its repercussions and many girls became widows even before they had attained the age of puberty. In some places they had to observe the cruel custom of Sati. But where Sati was not a universal practice, the widow was compelled to lead a forlorn life. She was deprived of the minimum comforts of life. She had to live on one meal a day, sleep on the floor and wear only borderless white saree. She was not allowed to grow hair on her head and look beautiful. She was considered inauspicious and bad omen of the society. Hence, she was not allowed to attend any functions. She was denied all home comforts and was doomed to a life of forced servility in the family in which during the lifetime of her husband, she most probably ruled as a queen. In the words of Behramji Malabari, a staunch advocate of widow-marriages. Sati was a single act of martyrdom or heroism, as the victim conceived it, and an act of religious merit as popularly believed, while the life which caste imposed on an unwilling widow was a perpetual agony, a burning to death by slow fire without any chastening or elevating effect on the suffer or any moral advantage to the community at large by way of compensation. She was rescued from the flames and was condemned to undergo her life sentence of rigorous imprisonment. No wonder, faced with such an alternative, many a widow had eagerly embraced the flames and became a Sati inspite of the law prohibiting it.

Thus the condition of a widow in Hindu society was unfortunate and miserable even to this day. Hence, there was a great need to reform this evil custom and improve the life of innocent girls. Pioneers like Kandukuri and many others worked hard to improve the status of unfortunate girl children.

Despite strong opposition from all sides, the first widow remarriage was performed in 1881 at Rajahmundry. The couple being Gogulapati Sriramulu and Gavaramma. Four days later, the second widow remarriage between Ratnamma and Ramachandra Rao took place. In 1884 a society for widow remarriage was started. By 1901, this Society performed thirty three widow remarriages. They were continued by Kandukuri's followers and other ardent reformers like Chilakamarthi Lakshminarasimham of Rajahmundry and Unnava Lakshminarayana of Guntur.

Devadasi System

Another despicable system that was predominant in Andhra was that of devadasis, specially from the sixteenth century onwards. In the 19th century it had become an in-thing for men to visit the devadasis. They used to spend a lot of money on them which ultimately impoverished and ruined their families. Besides there were many devadasis who shunned this type of life. Though highly talented in many arts, most of them had to expose themselves in obscene ways. While many girls wanted to lead a normal life, it became impossible for them to move in the normal society as they were not welcomed by it.

Pandit Madan Mohan Malaviya condemned this practice as a monstrosity and religious crime. Concerted efforts were made by the social reformers to eradicate this system, as devadasis who were highly talented would really be an asset to the society and could play a very useful part in the freedom struggle.

Veeresalingam Panthulu was the first social reformer in Andhra Predesh who agitated against the system of devadasi. He exposed the evils of this degrading system through satires, articles and pamphlets.

Raghupati Venkataratnam Naidu carried further the work initiated by Veeresalingam Pantulu. His social purity and anti-nautch movement roused public enthusiasm and hastened reformation. These efforts were continued later on by Darsi Chenchaiah.

There was by then great awakening among the devadasi community itself. Yamini Purnatilakam belonging to Kalavantulu family reacted at the degrading status of the Kalavantula community in society and openly condemned this evil. Gandhiji too continued the efforts of his predecessors. This evil custom came to an end with the Bill that was introduced and passed in 1937 and 1947 respectively, due to the efforts of Ammanna Raja and Dr. Muthu Lakshmi Reddy.

Dowry System

The *Kanyasulka* or bride's money lured greedy parents to get their young daughters married even to old men if they could get a good an amount sum in the bargain. There were a number of stories depicting the plight of these young girls. Gurajada Apparao's "*Puttadibomma Purnamma*" is a classic example of *Kanyasulkam*. He tried to highlight and prevent this evil practice to a large extent. His book "*Kanyasulkam*" became very popular. It was staged in every corner of the State. It became more popular after it was filmed. A full bench consisting of Chief Justice Sir Arnold While and Justices Miller and Munoe ruled that a contract to make payment to a father in consideration of giving daughter in marriage is immoral and opposed to public policy within the meaning Sec. 23 of the Indian Contact Act. Under orders of His Highness the Maharaja of Vizianagaram, a list was prepared sometime around 1887 of Brahmin Sulka marriages performed in Vizianagaram district during the year. The number of marriages recorded reached one thousand and thirty four during the year. This practice was followed by "*Vara Sulka*" money given along with the girl which had changed the fortune of the girl to the worse. The greed of the groom and his parents reached the Himalayan peak and any amount of offering was not sufficient. As the money given did not satisfy the groom's parents, the lot of the bride even after marriage caused serious concern. Even today this evil practice is persisting in many families. The parents of these girls are never in peace, because the in-laws of the girl continuously demand money or gifts even after marriage and there is a constant threat to the life of the girl.

Various organisations were responsible for the eradication of these social evils to a large extent. The reform movements started in the nineteenth century as a result of contact of indigenous culture with the Western culture. Western culture however had its influence only on the progressive intelligentsia. In the beginning of the twentieth century, the irresistible forces of nationalism, liberalism and egalitarianism imposed a new pattern of outlook on the people whose quickened awareness manifested itself in their concerted action in the political and social fields. The year 1900 which marks the quickening of the awareness had been taken as the starting point. The subsequent years had witnessed the mergence of several forces which helped in carrying on the reform work initiated in the previous century, to fulfill and provide an impetus that was necessary for this country to emerge as a democratic and progressive nation.

Social Reform Movement in the 19th Century

The social reform movement of the 19th century is an outcome of the British Government's policies and programmes in India. To overcome the impact of the Western influences the educated Indian elite, especially men undertook the programmes of reform of their customs and social practices. In this process, women became central to the social reform movement by giving them access to education through eradication of social evils and practices which affected women's status in society. In the long run women also became central to the reform movement as active participants. The reform movement has been regarded as a key to the intellectual processes that went into the making of modern India. It is said that no other coherent body of thought so sensitively and profoundly exposed the mental processes of an Indian as they formulated the ideas underlying the structure of their modern society as did the literature on social reform".

Beginning of Social Reform

The stimulus for social reform is traced to the Western ideas, English education and the onslaught of Christianity on Hinduism. Early 19th century is marked by a gap in the status of men and women. This gap is clearly evident in the denial of education to women, early marriage, polygamy, the rites of Sati, denial of property rights and practice of Purdah. From this, it can be inferred that the condition of women was pitiable. In contrast, men had access to Western education through English medium. The educated Indian elite was also exposed to the egalitarian ideals of western liberal thought of French philosophers and British Utilitarians. At about the same time, Christian Missionaries began to criticise the inadequacies of Indian culture and Hindu religion.

The newly educated male elite were thereby products of the new system of English education, though some came from traditional system. All the scholars had mastery over one or more of the major philosophical and religious systems. They were resentful of the attack on Hinduism by the Christian Missionaries and were ashamed of the degeneration of its culture.

Academicians who bestowed attention on the social reform movement observe that of the three cultural systems absorbed by the 19th century reformers the Hindu system perhaps retained or demonstrated the maximum ambivalence between matriarchy and patriarchy.

Veena Majumdar remarked on the 19th century social reformers thus: they were concerned by the impact of modernisation that increased the gap between men and women and threatened the stability of the family sought to strengthen women's" position with education and limited rights to property". Towards this end they tried to graft ideas from the West on to the existing culture and to defend it against Western criticism. As a result socio-cultural movement in colonial India showed contradictions. As M.N. Srinivas has put it, there was ambivalence in the elite "towards their own society" and towards the British.

Issues of Social Reform

The ambivalence of the elite towards their own society and towards the British perhaps accounts for the lack of unanimity and homogeneity in their aspirations and objectives. However, common to all of them is their pre-occupation with problems that affected women of their own social class that made them vulnerable to humiliation. To illustrate, Raja Ram Mohan Roy's own experience of the death of his brother's wife which led him to take up the cause of widow remarriage with such fanatic zeal have been recorded and that of many British officers.

The issues which attracted the social reformers were Sati, the ill-treatment of widows and the ban on widow remarriage, polygamy, child marriages and denial of property rights and education of women. Accepting women's status within the family as an index of their own progress and modernity, the earlier reformers criticised particularly inhuman practices like widow immolation (sati), marriage of child brides to much older men, ban on remarriage of widows, and sought to promote some form of education for women. Orthodox criticism of such moves was countered by statements that such reforms would arrest conversions to Christianity or the drifts of oppressed widows to prostitution and strengthen the stability of the traditional patriarchal family.

Need for Social Reform

Social reformers felt that the social evils should be eradicated by raising consciousness and making people sensitive to the injustices perpetuated on women. They felt that by giving women access to education and by enacting progressive legislations, social change could be initiated. While the reformers were concerned with the oppressed conditions of women and wanted to improve their lot though legislation and arousing social conscience, their objectives did not include any conception of equality in the roles between men and women. They saw women as custodians of the family and responsible for the well being of children and for imparting values of Indian culture and civilisation and social change could be initiated. The reformers were concerned with the oppressed conditions of women and advocated reinstalling them on their honoured seat of ancient glory and splendour through legislation and arousing social conscience. They demanded the restoration of healthy and congenial conditions as existed in the early Vedic Period. Thus the Renaissance of Indian women attempted by social reformers exerted upon the democratisation of social relations and removal of harmful practices on the basis of revival of Vedic society which was considered to be truely democratic.

Social Reform Movements

A Galaxy of social reformers contributed a great deal for the emergence of a brilliant era of social reform in India through various organisations like the Brahma Samaj, Arya Samaj and the Ramakrishna Mission. Some of the eminent social reformers are Raja Ram Mohan Roy, Eshwara Chandra Vidya Sagar, Swami Dayananda Saraswati, Maharaj Rai Saligram Bahadur, Keshab Chandra Sen, Mahadev Govind Ranade, Dhondo Keshav Karve, Rabindranath Tagore, Swami Vivekananda, Sri Kandukuri Veeresalingam Pantulu, R. Venkata Ratnam Naidu, Gopala Krishna Gokhale and Mahatma Gandhiji.

The British conquest and its rule over India in the 19th century brought about a transformation of Indian economy as well as society. The new land revenue settlements, commercial agriculture and infrastructure facilities like roads, railways, postal and telegraph services etc ushered in by British led to a significant change in the Indian village economy. The Indian economy became a colony to Britain primarily sub serving the needs of the later. The new economic system and administrative machinery required a new type of educated personnel which resulted in the establishment of Western educational institutions in India which imparted modern Western education. The Indians who were the beneficiaries of the new economic system of British in India were attracted towards Western education, as a result a new class of intelligential trained in modern Western sciences and culture evolved in the Indian society. The articulate Intelligentsia became the pioneers of all progressive democratic movements—social, political, economic and cultural. Of all the activities important movements of this group, emancipation of Indian women or the emergence of Indian women's movement is more significant.

On the eve of the British rule in India, eight principal social evils i.e Sati, female infanticide, Polygamy, Child Marriage, Purdah, absence of education among women, devadasi and the joint family system degraded the position of Indian women. There were two groups of social reformers i.e Liberal reformers and the revivalists. Both the groups undoubtedly recognised the oppressive social institutions and customs of India. But the former groups on the basis of liberal philosophy put forth their work for the cause of women whereas the latter groups work is based on a programme of the revival at the Vedic society in modern India. While arguing in favour of equal rights for women appealed to logic, reason, history, the principal of individual freedom and the requirements of social programme, social reformers such as Raja Ram Mohan Roy, Keshab Chandra Sen, Eswarachandra Vidyasagar, Swami Dayanand Saraswathi and others had provided leadership to the women's movement by frankly acknowledging the degraded position of Indian women. The social reformers concentrated their attention on important aspects of women like sati, age of marriage, the sad plight of widows and their right to remarry. The social reformers established a number of societies like Bramho Samaj, Prarthana Samaj, Ramakrishna Mission and others for the cause of Indian women. The best exponent of liberalism was Raja Ram Mohan Roy from Bengal. He was the first Indian in modern times to initiate social reform movement and champion for the cause of women. He advocated equality between the two sexes and declared that women were not inferior to men morally and intellectually.

The practice of female infanticide was already declared illelgal by the British Government through Regulations of 1795 and 1804. Roys attention was therefore drawn towards the next crying evil, the inhuman practice of Sati. His own sister-in-law was a victim of Sati and he could see with his own eyes the extent of barbarism involved in this cruel custom. From 1818 onwards he began active propaganda through speeches and writings against Sati. He boldly declared that the practice had no support in the *sastras*. Largely because of his effort and persuasion, the East India Company declared the Sati practice illegal and punishable offence in 1829 and the act is known as *Sati Prohibition Act*.

Raja Ram Mohan Roy also opposed other evils like early marriage, polygamy and *Kulinism* (a practice prevalent in Bengal by which lower caste girls were married to upper caste men to enhance the family status). Sometimes on kulin man will take several wives because of the attraction of dowry on one side and absence of conjugal responsibilities on the other. Raja Ram Mohan Roy supported female education, widow remarriage and intercaste marriage. He wanted that women should have the right of inheritance and property. In 1822, he prepared and published a pamphlet on "Brief remarks on modern encroachments on the ancient rights of women". Roy founded Brahmo Samaj which played a significant role in the reform activities concerning women. He founded Brahmo Samaj with a view to carry on the reform activities on a more systematic basis.

The Brahmo Samaj, soon after its inception became a vigorous social reform movement first in Bengal and then it quickly spread to other parts of the country and added to the volume and strength of similarly aimed local movements which had begun to rise in these places during this time. As the pioneer movement, Brahmo Samaj had also large interactions with local reformist groups. The members of the Brahmo Samaj opposed the caste system and social discrimination and they concentrated greatly on improving the low conditions of women and played a very important role in the introduction of several beneficial measures.

Raja Ram Mohan Roy saved widows from immolation on the funeral pyres of their husbands while Eshwara Chandra Vidya Sagar released them from living death by helping to legalise the widow remarriage. The evil of child marriage resulted in large number of young girls ending up as widows whose life was miserable due to the restrictions imposed on them. He argued in favour of widow remarriage on the basis of *Parasara Sanhita* and published his work on Widow remarriage in 1853.

Arya Samaj was established by Dayanand Saraswathi in 1875. Dayanand Saraswathi emphasised compulsory education for both boys and girls. A series of schools for Women—*Arya Kanya Patasals*—which later on developed into college was the first concerted effort of the Samaj to promote women's education in a systematic way. Prarthana Samaj was founded by some Maharashtra Brahmins in 1867. Its leaders were M.G. Ranade, N.G. Chandrasarkar and R.G. Bhandarkar. It concentrated more on sponsoring education for women. Some of its leading members were however active in the cause of women. Both Brahmo Samaj and Prarthana Samaj made forceful efforts to prove that Hindu religious tradition was not the source of legitimacy for the sorrowful condition of women in society. Under the influence of the liberal thought of the west, the two Samaja's strove restore to women to their dignified status.

The efforts of Vidya Sagar, Keshab Chandra Sen and D.K. Karve resulted in the enactment of widow remarriage act of 1856 which permitted widows to remarry if they born of such marriage. In the South, Kandukuri Veerasalingam led the widow remarriage movement. In 1874, he performed 63 widow remarriages throughout Madras presidency. He supported financially the men who got married widows by providing them houses and other means.

Another aspect of women's life death by the reformers was the age of girls at marriage. In the 19th century the average age of marriage for girls was 8 or 9. The extensive propaganda by Vidya Sagar and other reformers in this regard led the British government to legislate in order to improve the condition of minor girls and the Age of Consent Bill was passed in 1860 which made sexual intercourse with a girl of less than 10 years of age as rape. Further social reformers like Mahadev Govind Rande, Behramji Malabari and Tej Bahadur Sapru in their attempts to further raise the age of marriage cited several cases of consummation at the age of 10 or 11 which led to serious physical and psychological disturbances. Behramji, a parsi Journalist published his notes on "infant marriage and enforced widowhood" in 1884 suggesting certain reforms to be adopted in the educational institutions to discourage child marriage and also suggested some measures to the Government to improve the condition of widows. It was between 1884 and 1889 that enormous pressure was brought to bear on the government to enact law to further raise the age at marriage of the girl child. At last due to the collective efforts of the reformers in 1891, the Bill known as the age of consent was passed, which raised the marriageable age of girls to 12 years.

The social reformers felt that through female education the social evils that were linked to the issue of preserving and strengthening basic family structure could be eliminated and good wives and mothers could emerge from the same. Starting from Raja Ram Mohan Roy including the liberal as well as orthodox reformers supported female education. This resulted in the establishment of schools for girls and homes for widows. Eswara Chandra Vidya Sagar established Bethune school in 1849 along with Bethune, member of the Victory's committee which later on was turned into the famous Bethune College. Between 1855 and 1858 while he was working as an inspector of schools, Vidya Sagar had established 48 girls schools. To prevent the girls from attending the school, as there was a financial obstacle, Vidya Sagar supplied all the necessary materials for the education of girls. M.G. Ranade along with his wife propagated the female education and started girls high school in 1884. The limited enforcement and practicability of legislations like widow remarriage act of 1856 and others in a tradition bound society was recognised by Karve, who therefore concentrated his efforts on promoting education among widows. In 1896 Karve along with 15 of his colleagues founded the Ananth Balikashram for the education of widows, where the courses were drawn up with an idea to make the widows self -reliant. He alo started Mahila Vidyalaya in 1907 and S.N.D.T. women's University at Bombay in 1916, a separate educational institution for women so as to lesson the resistance of orthodox section with regard to women's education. The social reform movement in its later phases resulted in producing women social reformers who worked for their own cause. Pandita Ramabai started Sharda Sadan in Bombay in 1889 to provide an ashram to destitute high caste widows. In 1912-1913 a widows home was established by sister Subbulakshmi, another widow in Madras.

Another important aspect of the social reform movement phase of women's movement in India was that of property rights for Hindu women. The existing practice was particularly harsh on the Hindu widow who had no claim on her husband property except the right at maintenance as a result of which she was at the mercy of her husbands relatives. Raja Ram Mohan Roy suggested that the government should enact and enforce laws to remove these disabilities of women and bring economic freedom and self-reliance to them. As a result of efforts of the Brahmo Samaj, special marriage act of 1872 with its provision for divorce and succession to property to women was passed. The married women's property act of 1874 widened the scope of *stridhan* (Women's property) and expanded the right to own and acquire property by women. It also gave a widow a life interest in her husband's share of the property and a share equal to that of a son.

Swami Vivekananda, Swami Dayananda Saraswati and Annie Besant were the prominent reformers of the revivalist group who also worked for the cause of Indian women. The degradation of women's status in Indian society is the result of the deviations from the customs and traditions. Swami Vivekananda, Dayananda Saraswati and Annie Besant were worked for the prominent who are in Indian society and of the ancient Vedic society of the Hindus. So this group believed in the revival of the Vedic society in modern India. Dayanand Saraswati, the founder of Arya Samaj was against child marriage. Dayanand encouraged widow remarriages and realised the tragic plight of widows and hence set up several rescue homes and orphanages. Annie Besant leader of the theosophical movement was also against child marriage and supported remarriage of child widows. She laid emphasis on the importance of female education. Though revivalists wanted to revive the Vedic society, they fought for women's rights in various aspects, thus added strength to the social reform movement.

The Muslim women in India made little progress in their position both in the pre British period or later British period. Western education, the major vehicle of progress during the British period did not reach them partly because of the existence of Purdah and seclusion of women from external environment and partly, because education was considered essential for them. Even male Muslims were slow to accept english education. As a result, educated Muslims formed only a small segment of the population in the 19th century and were confined to urban areas in the county. Consequently, efforts in education and association formation among muslim women did not begin until the 20th century and one notable exception was the Tyabji family of Bombay. Badruddin Tyabji who graduated from the elphinstone college founded a muslim self-help association in 1876. His female relatives were later active in starting a Muslim girls school (Amina Binte Badruddin Tyabji) running a girls orphanage (Begum Nawale Misra) and starting nursing centers (Shareefa Hamid Ali).

Thus the social reformers laid the foundation of the women's movement in India. Social reform movement was the first attempt to remove the obstacles in the life of women. It created awareness among the people that women must be liberated and be made equal of men. The several organisations established by them also continued the women's movement. Ranade's Indian National Social Conference shifted the women's movement from individual to small groups, to national plans.

National Movement

As a result of the social reform movement of the 19th century, the social evils were eliminated and opportunities were provided to women for their education. The expansion of women's education and their admission to educational institutions had produced a sizable number of english educated middle class women by the late 19th century and they made their presence felt in political activities. The characteristics of the second phase of women's movement i.e. the national movement are that for the first time limited number of women belonging to the elite section of Indian society started taking part in the political activities. Till 1919, the national movement was limited to the urban middle class and it was later only with Gandhiji's entrance into the national movement, participation of the masses began to take place. In this phase, political developments and women's participation in the National movement went hand in hand. Besides, women's movement national movement continued simultaneously.

The partition of Bengal in 1905 resulted in the launching of Swadeshi movement by the nationalists. Though there was the absence of mass awakening amongst the women, but there was some sort of movement spreading slowly in them. Meetings were arranged and khadi spinning were taken up by women. Women contributed their bangles, nose rings and bracelets to the national fund. In villages, women started putting away a handful of grain daily for such purpose. The women workers of the Arya Samaj were also responsible for arousing national spirit among the people. Swarna Kumari, sister of Rabindranath Tagore and her daughter Salara Devi were strong supporters of swadeshi movement. Important women who participated in the revolutionary activities were Shyamji Krishna Varma, Nauroji, grand daughter of Dadabhai Nauroji, Ms.M.Chettorpadhya, sister of Narendranath Chattopadhyaya, Madam Bhikamji Rustum and K.R. Kame who was one of the prominent leaders of the revolutionary party in Europe.

The Swadeshi period marked the formation of several women's Organisations. Sarala Devi took steps to organise women's movement and its nucleus in the form of Bharat Stri Maha Mandali was formed in Lahore in 1910. Branches of this organisation were established at Allahabad and Calcuttta. The objective of this society was to bring together the women of all castes and creeds on the basis of their economic interests in the moral and material progress of women in India. Parvati Devi, the headmistress of the Hindu girls school at Kanchi, a small town in the Madras presidency started Kanchi Mahila Parishad to equip women of Kanchi with an idea of affairs of state and to create a public opinion over burning issues before the nation.

Another society known as Gujarati Hindu Stri Mandal was started in Bombay. Thus various women's organisations came into being from time to time during the national movement.

During the early decade of the 19th century Dr. Annie Besant and Sarojini Naidu who became political as well as women's movement's leaders latter on appeared on the political scene. The period from 1911-18 is of great significance in the history of Indian national movement because for the first time a woman, Annie Besant led the national movement as president of Indian National Congress. The setting up of Home Rule League and organisation of the Home Rule agitation which took the Nation from the deep slumber had raised the tempo of national movement. In the history of women's movement these years are important. It was due to the lead given by Annie Besant that organised movement for the emancipation of women took place and the demand for political rights for women came to be firmly established on political agenda on the nations. The important achievement of the women's movement in India during the second phase was the founding of Women's Indian Association (WIA).

The Women's Indian Association was founded in 1917 by Annie Besant and Margaret Cousins an Irish feminist who came to India in 1915 and Dorothy, Jinara Jadasa's wife of Srilanka theosophist. In 1927 it had 43 branches and 2,300 members and increated to 80 branches and 4,000 members by 1937. It was mainly concerned with influencing the government policy on women's suffrage, educational and social reforms issues. Its main objectives were creating awareness among women as daughters of India, highlighting the role of wives and mothers in training, guiding and forming the character of the future rulers of India, spread of women's education, elimination of child marriage and other social evils, franchise for women and establishment of equality of rights between men and women. This association played an important role in articulating the women's movement till its merger with the All Women's India Conference (AWIC).

From the beginning, the Indian women's movement approached the suffrage campaign as a measure of achieving social reform. The leaders believed that the enfranchisement of women would mean additional support for reform legislation. Margaret Cousins was the first person to raise the issue of women's franchise and a delegation was sent to meet Montagu, the secretary of state under the leadership of Sarojini Naidu. The delegation appeared before Montage in 17 December 1917. The memorandum asked for women's franchise on the same basis as men in the new constitution and improved facilities for women's education and health care. The delegation consisted of 18 Indian women and 4 European women from various organisations such as the women's Indian Association, the Seva Sadan and the Senate of Indian Women's University. Three European women in the delegation i.e. Besant, Cousins and Jinara Jadasa had participated in the women's suffrage movement in Britain. The initial reaction of both the British authorities and Indian elite to the women's suffrage demand was negative. However, the Indian elite late agreed to support the demand.

The entry of Gandhiji with his experience in South Africa altered the national politics dramatically. He realised the importance of mass base to Indian nationalism and subsequently an ideology which suited the same was introduced. Gandhian style of mass mobilisation had implications for the Indian women's movement is as much as increasing number of women were sought to be mobilised for participation in the independent movement. Even though Gandhiji recognised the existence of a set of problems unique to women, he saw no conflict between a women's movement and a national movement. Gandhiji's view of women's equality was located within a religious sense of the word and within the confines of patriarchal system with a ring of religiosity about it projecting a concept of women's role as being complementary to that of men and embodying virtues of sacrifice and suffering. During the Gandhian era of national movement, women continued their movement for political rights and social reform activities by forming into organisation.

Gandhiji had launched an all India Satyagraha in 1919 against the provocative enactment of the Rowlat Act. Women took out processions, propagated the use of Khadi and even courted jail. Though a few number of women were arrested, yet a beginning was made. Women gave up their ornaments, broke their foreign bangles and vowed that they would not wear that item again. Though the non-cooperation movement ended in failure, it awakened the women of all sections and imparted first lessons in satyagraha.

After the struggle for franchise, for the first time Indian women exercise their vote in the elections of 1926. The franchise granted to women was very restricted. In the elections 22 per cent women in Madras, 12 per cent in Bombay and Punjab, 9.6 per cent in Bengal and 4.5 per cent in Uttar Pradesh casted their votes. The first woman to stand for elections was Kamala Devi Chattopadhaya. Madras was the first state which nominated a woman member Dr. Muttu Lakshmi Reddy to the legislative council. She saw to the enactment of the abolition of devadasi system and for laws to close brothels and protect the minor girls. She brought amendments to the children's act and worked for the creation of health schools and children's ward.

A large number of women actively took part in the Dandi march, first and foremost among them was Sarojini Naidu. Women participated by breaking salt laws, forest laws taking out Pradhat pheries, Processions, Picketings at schools, colleges, legislative Councils and clubs. In 1931 Sajojini Naidu attended the second Round Table Conference as an official representative of the women of India.

During the civil disobedience movement of 1930, Kamla Devi Chattopadhyaya addressed meetings and picketed foreign cloth and liquor shops. She was in charge of women's organisation of the Hindustan Seva Dal. The inauguration of provincial autonomy under the act of 1935 gave Indian women an opportunity to be elected to the state legislatures and also become administrators. In the elections of 1937, eight (8) women were elected from the general constituencies, Forty two (42) from the reserved constituencies and Five (5) were nominated to the upper House when the ministries were formed, then(10) women took office one as minister and others as deputy speakers and parliamentary secretaries.

The Quit India movement which was the last in the series of nationalist agitation was launched by Gandhiji in 1942 with a significant slogan "Do or die". Men leaders were arrested in the first round up and in their absence women carried on the movement and bore the burnt of the British Wrath. The women not only took processions and held demonstrations but also organised camps in which they were given training in civil duties and first aid and were educated on democracy and Indian constitution. Women organised political prisoners relief fund and collected large amounts and some women went underground and directed the movement from there. In the Indian National Army of Subhash Chandra Bose, Rani Jhansi Regiment was created for women's Regiment. Women were trained in nursing, social service and to use rifles, bayonets, machine guns, revolvers, submachine guns, swords and daggers. Lakshmi Swaminathan was the commander of the Rani Jhansi regiment. Thus women took part in the various activities of the national movement. The specific feature of this phase of women's movement is that establishment of several specific women's organisations led by women themselves built up their own organisations on all India scale with a comprehensive programme of social, economic, cultural and political advancement of Indian women.

3

Role of Women in the Freedom Movement

Introduction

Despite the dualism in men's attitudes towards women's rules in the family and Society, rightly characterised by K.M. Panikkar as "Public Veneration and Private Humiliation", many women participated in the Freedom Movement by performing their domestic and social roles. The participation of Women in India's historic struggle for Freedom was a countrywide phenomenon. However, much of the literature on Freedom Struggle in India made only occasional references to women and did not adequately reflect the contribution of women. As Veena Muzumdar has rightly put it, "Existing research on Women and Indian Nationalism...be described as non-comprehensive, cursory in nature and generally a "history from above". So within the limitations of the existing literature one has to understand and analyse the role of women in India's Freedom Struggle.

The Freedom Movement covered a time-span of sixty-two years starting with the birth of the Indian National Congress in 1885 up to 1947. When India attained Independence women participated in the Movement during the entire period though the degree of participation varied across different stages of the

Movement. However, the actual participation of women in the freedom struggle began with the emergence of Gandhiji on the political scene of India in the 1920's.

In the course of the Freedom Movement, many women freedom fighters played an important role. So their individual efforts need to be reflected upon for a proper understanding of women's role in the freedom struggle.

Role of Women in the Freedom Struggle

For convenience, women's participation and role in the freedom struggle is analysed according to the major landmarks in the freedom struggle. The periodisation is as follows:

- Role of women from1885-1905
- Role of women from 1905-1919
- Role of women from 1919-1947

Prior to the establishment of the Indian National Congress, the first attempt at a national revolt against the British was made in the Revolt of 1857 in which women have played a vital role.

Rani Lakshmi Bai of Jhansi emerged as a great heroine during the revolt and her bravery and courage have immortalised her name. Other prominent women who participated in the 1857 revolt also known as Sepoy Mutiny were: Rani Tara Bai, Begum Hazrat Mahal, Lalitha Bakshi, Jhalkari, Sunder Kashi Bai, Munder Moti Bai, Rani of Ranigarh and Rani of Tulsipur. They may be few in number but they symbolised the spirit and qualities of Indian womanhood.

Role of Women from 1885-1905

The spirit of violent opposition, suppressed with British success in 1857 did not vanish. It smouldered in the hearts of people who were waiting for opportunity to spread out like wild fire. At this time in 1885, Indian National Congress emerged which provided a platform for all men and women to avenge their wrath against the British and achieve freedom for the country. Right from 1885 women were given membership to the Indian National Congress as the political reformers were aware of their worth.

Laying the foundation of Indian National Congress in 1885, Allan Octavian Home added that "the political' reformers of all shades of opinion should never forget that unless the elevation of the female element of the nation proceeds with equal pace with the work, all their labour for political enfranchisement will prove vain". Ten women attended the fourth session of the Congress at Bombay in 1889. Since 1900, the number gradually began to increase, when K. Ganguly, the first woman doctor of Bengal became the first woman to speak from the Congress Platform. Like the men, women participants who attended were from Calcutta and Bombay.

Amongst them was Swarna Kumari Devi, a great social reformer, the first Indian woman editor and sister of Rabindranath Tagore. Before joining the Indian National Congress Swarna Kumari started women's Association to foster among Indian women an active and enlightened interest in the welfare of the country. The other women present were Pandita Ramabai, Mrs. Shevanti Bai, Mrs. Shanti Bai N. Kamber, Mrs. Kashi Bai Kanitkar and Manikjee Arbtejee, all of whom became renowned educationists and social reformers.

The partition of Bengal in 1905 infused a new spirit of patriotism. Though there was no mass awakening amongst the women at this time, the elite women participants in the deliberation of the Indian National Congress began to shoulder responsibility in the national efforts through the press and platform.

The participants in the 1857 revolt mostly hailed from princely class. Those who joined the Indian National Congress are also elite women social reformers or educationists. Thus the participation of women during the early phase of the freedom struggle is limited to the upper class only and from that class also the number of participants were few.

Role of Women from 1905-1919

The role of women during this period varied form contributions of National fund publicity and protest, liaison between revolutionary leaders watched by policewomen contributed their gold bangles, nose rings and bracelets to the National Fund.

They were involved in diverse nationalist activities both within and outside the home. At home they spun and wove Khadi, held classes to educate other women and contributed significantly to nationalist literature in the form of articles, poems and propaganda material.

Women also played a significant role in maintaining illegal liaison among revolutionaries who are under the watchful eyes of the Police. Kumudini Mitter, daughter of Kristo Mitter, a renowned nationalist propagated the cult of revolution through Suprabhat, a Bengali Magazine. Sarala Devi, daughter of Swarna Kumari, a prominent social reformer and ardent worker of Swadeshi Cause and niece of great poet Rabindranath Tagore formed the link between Punjab and Bengal revolutionaries. She also opened "Lakshmi Bhandar" for popularising Swadeshi goods.

Sarala Devi Chaundurani became an accepted mobiliser of youth in the nationalist cause and was noted by official intelligence reports as far more dangerous to the Raj than her husband, a well-known revolutionarist. In 1901 she formed the Bharat Sri Mahamandal after serious differences with the male leadership of the National Social Conference.

Thus the emergence of an elite brand of women taking interest in the socio-political affairs of the country particularly after the partition of Benal in 1905, the Home Rule League of Annie Beasant, birth of women's Organisations established like Women's Indian Association (WIA), All India Women's Conference (AIWC) and Local Level Organisations in the facilitating factor.

The period 1914-1918 is significant in the history of the freedom struggle for two reasons. Firstly, it was for the first time that a woman Beasant led the movement and secondly, it was significant because her entry into politics in 1914 accelerated the process of women's association with the freedom struggle. It was due to the lead given by Annie Beasant that an organised movement for the emancipation of women and to put forward the demand for political rights for women came to be established.

Her leadership gave strength, encouragement and inspired Indian women to participate in the Freedom Struggle in large numbers. Thus she prepared the ground for Gandhian Freedom Movement in which women of all classes have played a prominent role.

Gandhiji and Role of Women

The emergence of Gandhiji on the political scene in the 1920's as the nationalist leader had tremendous impact on women. His ideas about women's roles in the Freedom Struggle were considered 'revolutionary' for that period. He was critical of those roles that affected women adversely like Purdah, dowry and the Devadasi (temple dancers) Tradition.

It is important to discuss how Gandhiji envisaged the participation of women in nationalist politics. He realised the significant role of women could play in the Freedom Struggle by their active participation. He argued that the qualities of self-sacrifice and 'silent suffering' were deep-rooted in Indian women. Thus women were ideally suited to participate in the movement, the core concepts of which are *Ahimsa* (non-violence in thought, action and deed) and *Satyagraha*. If non-violence is the law of our being, the future is with women.

Gandhiji thus stressed those qualities of women, which were beneficial for the political campaign. An integral feature of Gandhiji's Civil Disobedience Movement and one for which women were particularly suited was spinning and weaving Khadi. Gandhiji advocated self-reliance by weaving one's own cloth and boycotting foreign cloth. Sarala Devi Sarabhai, an activist acknowledged her motivation to join the Nationalist Movement as a desire to fulfil her dharma.

Spinning on the Charka (Spinning Wheel) was an integral part of Gandhiji's construction programme and his campaign against the colonial masters. Spinning and weaving Khadi enhanced the significance of women's contribution to the movement in their own eyes. Also the more tradition bound of which women could have the satisfaction of participating without going on the street was on move.

Role of Women During the Period 1919-1922

Women from different parts of the country joined the processions and propagated the use of Khadi and Charka. Some of them left Government Schools and Colleges in Calcutta after listening to Gandhiji's speeches. Besanta Devi accompanied her husband, Deshbandhu Chitta Ranjan Das in his tours of Bengal and asked women to boycott foreign goods. Under her leadership women volunteers sold Khadi in the streets of Calcutta. Both Hindu and Muslim women contributed together for this success.

Role of Women During the Period 1922-1930

In the Bardoli Satyagraha of 1928, a no-tax campaign was launched under the leadership of Sardar Patel. The women of Bardoli took part in this movement from its very beginning. Women thronged his meetings with singing patriotic songs. The peasants of Bardoli were forced to leave their land, buffaloes and land confiscated, and household goods were auctioned. However, they refused to pay taxes. Throughout, the women supported their men-folk. Mithuben Patel and Mani Behn Patel and Bhakliben Desai fixed their tents and huts on the land declared to be sold by the Government.

Bardoli Satyagraha besides proving an eye opener to the people, displayed large measure of strength amongst women. It set new example as this was the first time that simple rural women participated in the freedom struggle though they belonged to the well-off peasant sections.

Civil Disobedience Movement 1930-1935

In the 1930's Gandhiji began to encourage the emergence of women into public space. In the year 1930, the pledge of Independence began in March. Gandhiji opened a new phase of Satyagraha by announcing that he would break the Salt Law. This activity received a greater eager response from women. Mahatma Gandhi started his historic March to Dandi on the seacoast near Jabalpur. On 12 March, 1930, as salt was a commodity that affected women from all walks of life, women all over the country marched to the sea depots to manufacture salt, an activity which was illegal.

During the second phase of the Civil Disobedience Movement women not only actively participated in movements for breaking Salt Laws, Forest Laws but some of them holding high positions have also resigned their jobs to protest against the high-handed measures of the Government. To illustrate Muthu Lakshmi Ammal resigned her seat in Legislative Council and her Office as Deputy President of the Council. Mrs. Hansa Mehta and Kamabba Lakshmana Rao resigned their Offices as honorary magistrates.

In Madhya Pradesh, women lost their lives in police firing in connection with defying of forest laws. This procession led by Smt. Swarup Rani Nehru, wife of Sri Motilal Nehru and was lathi charged. These incidents have activated women to participate in various Satyagrahas.

Many women in different parts of the country participated in large numbers in the Civil Disobedience Movement under the leadership of prominent women of those parts. Gandhiji nominated Sarojini Naidu to lead the raid on Dharasana after him and Abbas Tyabji were arrested. In Bombay, Kamala Devi Chattopadhyay and Avantibai Gokhale were the first women to break Salt laws. In Madras, Durgabai Deshmukh nominated by T. Prakasam and in Gujarat Mridula Sarabhai led the women Satyagrahas. A procession of 5000 women inaugurated the Civil Disobedience Movement in Punjab. Aparna Basu has mentioned the women of the Nehru family having responded to Gandhiji's call.

Not only Vijaya Lakshmi Pandit and Krishna but the aged Swarup Ram and the ailing Kamala were in the frontline of leadership, organising processions, addressing meetings and picketing foreign cloth.

A.V. Kuttimalu Amma, Kamala Prabhu, C. Kunhikavu Amma, Kunhi Lakshmi Amma, Margaret Pavamani, M.R. Janaki Amma and Iswari Amma had been the earliest to lead the Satyagraha and the Non-Violent Agitation in Kerala. The political organisations such as Rashtreeya Stree Sabha, Kerala Desa Sevika Sangh and Swadeshi Committee took the lead in popularising the motto of Civil Disobedience Movement by organising classes in spinning, popularising Hindi, propagation of prohibition and by offering training programmes in crafts for women.

Civil Disobedience Movement During 1935-1947

The individual civil disobedience movement and the Quit India Movement of August 1942 mark the last phase of the freedom struggle. During this phase, both the elite and the ordinary women courted arrest through participation in satyagrahas and individual civil disobedience movements in various states. Those who could not agree to Gandhiji's creed on non-violence helped revolutionary leaders and also turned themselves into revolutionaries.

Among the women leaders, Sucheta Krupalani who was in-charge of the women's department of the All India Congress Committee (AICC) since 1939 was one of the first person to court arrest in the individual civil dis-obedience movement inaugurated by Gandhiji in October 1940.

The arrest of Gandhiji and other important leaders of the "Quit India Movement" in 1942, sparked off women's participation in large numbers in processions holding meetings and demonstrations and organising strikes in almost all the states of India.

In Assam, Kanakalatha Barua, a young girl in her teens played a memorable role in Quit India Movement in 1942. She led a procession of 500 women and marched to occupy the police warnings but boldly replied to the office-in-charge of the police thana "unless the thana office and his men wanted to act as the servants of the people, they must clear out and allow the people to take procession in the place". She was fired in the chest, which killed her. One of the woman killed was pregnant.

The excess of police and military on peaceful marches resulted in the coming up of women's organisations under the leadership of Anupriya Barua and Sudhalata Dutta. It was in Assam that free India's fighting force was organised. Women joined this force, organised Red Cross First Aid parties and rendered services to workers and countrymen throughout the country.

The thousand women of village Balaji came out on 7 October, 1942 to meet at the local police station. On 26 January 1943 one thousand women gathered to celebrate the Independence Day at a prayer meeting which was disturbed by the police.

In Bengal, the people of Midnapore District played a notable part in 1942 movement. The Tamalouk sub-division had organised itself against the Japanese invasion. A Khadi centre with four thousand spinners, where majority of women were organised. The women of Tamalouk division also took out processions and in one of these processions seven women were arrested and sentenced to two years of rigorous imprisonment. One such procession was led by a 73 year-old woman Smt. Manangini Hazee, to occupy Thana. She lost her life in police firing. Seventy four women of the division are victims of rape by Government employees. One of them died as a result of the assault, women with daggers tried to offer resistance collectively which proved effective.

The women organised Bhagini Seva Sangh to protect their honour and chastity in the wake of Government atrocities against women participants in the processions. Women also faced the soldiers and police with weapons. Two leaders were prosecuted under the Arms Act for dragging out daggers in self-defence.

Punjab energetically responded to the call of Mahatma Gandhiji. Out of the 104 students arrested at Lahore on 10 November 1942, twenty-two are girls. They were courageous and distributed badges in the presence of police. Raj Kumari Amrit Kaur played a leading role in organising processions and protest meetings. She was the most active person during Quit India Movement in 1942. She led the processions day after day. One such procession was subjected to ruthless lathi charge in Shimla. She was arrested at Calcutta and suffered a lot in the unhygienic conditions of the jail. Manmohini Sehgal, Parvati Devi, Lakshmi Devi, Amar Kaur and Pushpa Gujral were the women freedom fighters who raised the banner of patriotism in Punjab.

In Madhya Pradesh, women approached officials and members of the bar on Raksha Bandan Day with requests to resign and to refrain from attending courts, women of village Chimu of this province suffered the worst in the hands of 200 European soldiers and fifty Indian constables. Anasuya Bai Kale jumped into active politics during the Quit India Movement. Due to the efforts, the lives of twenty five young men associated with Astechimur chapter of the annals of the freedom struggle of 1942 were saved. Bombay was the first province to be affected by the political upsurge as it was in the vanguard of the freedom struggle. In Bombay Sarojini Naidu, Kasturba Gandhi, Hansa Mehta and Mrudula Sarabhai played an important role during the last phase of the freedom struggle.

Sarojini Devi was arrested on 3 December 1940 for taking part in the individual Satyagraha inaugurated by Vinoba Bhave. She was again arrested immediately after passing the Quit India Resolution on 9 August 1942. She appeared in public on 7 January 1944 and addressed a meeting at Bombay and Punjab. Government served a notice to her, prohibiting her from making any public speech or taking part in processions or writing to the newspapers after she reached Lahore Railway station in January 1944.

Kamaladevi Chattopadhyaya was arrested for her political work many times during 1939-1944. She visited U.S.A. to acquaint U.S. citizens about the conditions in India. Miraben was arrested during the Quit India Movement and was confined to Aga Khan palace for twenty one months. In Bombay one of the most dramatic episodes was the role played by Usha Mehta who operated an underground radio station. The "Congress Radio" news broadcast at 7-30 in the evening from August to November 1942 was made by Usha Meta till she was arrested with her colleague. She was sentenced to four years rigorous imprisonment and sent to Yerawada Jail.

In Karnataka, girl student took active part in the movement. At Dharwar on 23 October, 1942, two girl students, Hemalatha Shenalikar and Gulvadi entered the district courts and hoisted the tricolour flag on the judge's seat. Gulvadi addressed the members of the Bar exhorting them to support the cause of Independence. Balamakki Bamakka, the old mother of two influential merchants led a procession with a flag and Gandhiji's photo. She was also arrested.

Likewise women participated in different parts of the country particularly during the last phase of the freedom struggle. Among the women leaders who played important role in the 1942 movement are Sucheta Kripalani, Tarakeswari Sinha, Aruna Asaf Ali, Rajendra Kumari Bajpai, Nandini Satpathi, Begum Habibullah and Indira Gandhi. All of them led processions, addressed meetings and suffered imprisonment.

While women joined the freedom movement in large numbers at the call of Gandhiji there were a few who could not accept his creed of non-violence. Some of those women joined in the Indian National Army. Since the formation of Indian Independence League on 16 January 1942 at Kaulalumpur, Indian women in East Asian Countries helped to further the cause of India's Independence League, Indian women arrested in the preparation and collection of bandages, first field dressings, collection of funds and articles required by the troops and inspiring young men and women to do their duty at the critical hour.

In March 1943, when the women's section of Indian Independence League was inaugurated, Mrs. M.K. Chidambaram and Miss Saraswathi were elected as Chairman and Secretary of the women's section of league at Singapore. Dr. Lakshmi Swaminathan was appointed as secretary at the Head Quarters. In 1943, inspired by Subhash Chandra Bose's call to women to be ready to share the burden of the battle for freedom, women's regiment popularly known as "Rani Jhansi Regiment" was made. They were keen to go on active service. The first batch of this regiment was sent to Maymo (Burma). In the beginning of 1945, though they could not take part in actual fighting as the Indian National Army was retreating at that time.

Factors Influencing Women's Participation in the Freedom Struggle

Women participated in the struggle for freedom since the outbreak of Sepoy Mutiny in 1857. Their participation increased with the passage of time and entry of leaders like Mahatma Gandhiji and several others. The factors influencing women's participation in the struggles and the actual role played by them need recaptulation as it spread over almost sixty-two years.

Impact of Social Reform Movement

The reform movements carried on during 1800 to 1884 by the social reformers to improve the status of women and enactment of many Acts towards this goal had their impact. All the developments before the turn of the century, undoubtedly had a powerful impact upon the educated women of that period filling them with a sense of purpose. These elite women are attracted towards the freedom struggle to start with.

Family Influence

One major factor influencing women's participation in the freedom struggle was the involvement and imprisonment of their family members, parents, husbands or brothers. Women from families such as those of Motilal Nehru, D.R. Das, Jamanlal Bajaj and Lala Lajpat Rai naturally wanted to share the suffering of their men-folk. This is true not only of elite class but even among ordinary women-folk, whose husbands/sons/brothers are involved or imprisoned.

Home atmosphere also played an important role. There the home atmosphere is nationalistic and the women also imbibed it. To illustrate, Bina Das's father was a teacher and friend of Subhash Bose, Kamala Das Gupta's father was connected with Swadeshi Movement in Bengal. This is true of many other women leaders of prominence in the freedom struggle.

Literature

Books played their part in inspiring women towards struggle for freedom. Mrs. Annie Beasant's autobiography influenced Kamala Devi. Novels such as Saratchandra Chatterjee's "Pather Dabi" inspired some of the Bengali revolutionaries.

Inspiring Leadership

Charismatic and inspiring personalities had their sway over women's involvement into the movement. It is said that Dhiresh Majumdar, a student leader exercised great influence over the young girls who joined extremist groups in Calcutta. Similar is the Surya Sen's influence in Chittagong. Leaders like Subhash Chandra Bose in Bengal, Vallabhai Patel in Gujarat, Rama Manohar Lohia, Jawaharlal Nehru and above all Gandhiji were influential in drawing women into the freedom struggle. The biographies and autobiographies and women in Nationalist Movement amply reflect on the tremendous impact of Gandhiji on them.

Favourable Environment

The general environment also favoured women's participation in the freedom struggle. The patriotic slogans and processions particularly since the ushering of Civil Disobedience Movement in 1930 was such that women could hardly escape from participation. Genuine conviction, patriotic emotion and regard for local leaders and above all Mahatma's appeal to the women to be partners in the struggle for Swaraj provided conducive environment for women's participation.

Projection of Women's Issues as Part of the Nationalist Movement

The question of suffrage for women taken up by Nationalists brought women to the common platform. Gandhiji's realisation of the negative consequences of colonial rule on women's status and his decision to launch the Khadi movement which would offer to the masses of women an immediate open channel for their participation in the national struggle was an important motivating factor for many women to jump into the struggle since the starting of the civil disobedience movement calling Khadi mainly as a women's movement, unleashed women's aspirations to break through Purdah and other barriers of inequality. Similarly the incorporation of gender equality in the Fundamental Rights Resolution of 1931 is another step of significance in drawing mass of women into the struggle.

Another important aspect of women's participation in the freedom struggle was during the early period that it was limited to urban areas and therein to the educated classes. Most of the early participants came from a middle class background. They were professionals, businessmen and educated classes. The widening of the scope of the nationalist movement brought into its ranks – industrial workers and certain sections of peasantry. Patidar peasant women in Ras, Borsa, Bardoli, Karadi and Malwad were active in the Satyagraha Movement in these areas. Midnapur was politically more conscious and that village women actively participated in the freedom struggle. In 1930, unsophisticated village women marched side by side with women of Nehru family at Allahabad and Ahmedabad. Some Muslim women shed their Purdah and few Parsi women also joined the movement under Gandhiji's leadership, While many participated in Salt Satyagraha only a few brave women like Aruna Asaf Ali, Sucheta Kripalani and Usha Mehta carried on underground activities.

Women's Movements After Post Independence Period

Women's movement is the organised effort to achieve a common goal of equality and liberation of women and it presupposes sensitiveness to crucial issues affecting the life of women. For a concerted action to move towards the objective, there has to be some unifying ideological thread for various units. In analysing women's movement, women's organisations and groups provide significant structures through which the goals are attempted to be achieved, women mobilised and ideology articulated. Hence women's organisations and groups are pivotal in understanding women's movement. In the context of Indian women's movement one could say that, there is a growing number of organisations realising the need for being sensitive to women's issues and incorporating them into their programmes. The imperatives of including women's issues and concerns at policy level, the amendment of rape or sati legislation as a result of pressure from the women's groups, lessening of resistance towards terms like 'feminism' or 'feminist', growing media coverage are indicative of prevalence of a very different situation in relation to women's problems then what was existing before the late sixties.

The last three decades have been marked by the growth and development of the women's movement in India. New issues have been raised, new methods are used for bringing awareness among women and different structures are appearing to mobilise women's voice and their feelings and needs. In fact International Women's Decade (1976-1985) provided a leverage to women's movement in India. In the pre-independence period, the women's movement was very much a part of the nationalist movement. The liberal approach to women's issues and overall middle-class urban leadership mark out as significant features of the first phase of women's movement. With independence, when the constitutional equality was guaranteed and the Central Social Welfare Board (1953) evolved grant-in-aid programmes for women's organisations, a period of acquiescence began. Achievement of freedom not only generated optimism, but it was felt that legal enactments against social evils and welfare oriented programmes for women would ensure gender equality. Recognition of the vital reality that a struggle is necessary for implementing the principles of gender equality was yet to come. Stereotyped activities by women's organisations and apathy towards crucial issues concerning women marked the period of first two decades after independence. During the sixties, though specific women's issues did not surface prominently, yet women were mobilised in large numbers and they joined the general struggles of the rural poor, tribals, industrial working-class and other mass movements. Participation of women in Chipko movement, Naxalbari movement, anti-price raise demonstrations, Nav Nirman Youth Movement in Gujarat and Bihar, rural revolt in Dhule district Maharashtra State and Telangana Movement provided a backdrop for the ensuing struggles on women's issues.

CHIPKO MOVEMENT

The Chipko movement, which focussed world attention on the environmental problems of the Alaknanda catchment area in the mid-Himalayas was a movement of the local people to inform forest contractors plainly and simply why trees should not be cut. The movement spoke of the people who were dependent on the land and their problems and soon became popular in the entire region. Today the Chipko movement is not confined to tree protection or plantation but concerns itself with the safety and preservation of the environment.

Depletion of natural resources on the one hand and increasing appropriation of the available resources for the benefit of a few had adversely affected India's rural environment during the last few decades. This is reflected in the declining area under forestry and increase in area susceptible to environmental problems like water and wind erosion, water logging, fall in groundwater table, pollution of natural water resources through fertiliser-pesticides run-off. Along with depletion of natural resources, there is also decline in the village common lands due to privatisation and unabated encroachments.

These emerging trends in environmental degradation have hit women very hard, particularly those of poorer strata, living in semi-arid and hilly areas. The unequal gender division of labour and unequal access to resources, knowledge and decision marking coupled with depletion of natural resources had its adverse effects on women. These gender effects, reflect in the form of greater time burden to fetch water, fuel and fodder, reduced incomes from gathered items, shift to less nutritious items of food consumption with adverse effects on the well being and health of women.

The seriousness of the gender vulnerability is more manifested in northern states with adverse female sex ratios, low levels of female literacy, greater seclusion of females and limited access to arable land compared to the southern region.

The negative effects of gender inequality and environmental degradation are challenged by women's groups and environmental groups, the former protesting against the gender bias in existing patterns of development and the latter on the high environmental costs. Because of the women-nature linkage, women have been on the forefront in major environmental movements all over particularly in Third World Countries where the problems are felt more acutely compared to the west.

According to Vandana Shiva, women's environmental action in India preceded the UN women's decade as well as the 1972 Stockholm Environmental Conference. She traced the recorded history of the noted Chipko movement to three hundred years back when 300 members of the Bishnoi community led by Amrita Devi sacrificed their lives to save their khejri trees by climbing them.

The recent Chipko movement has popularly been referred to as women's movement. The history of Chipko is a history of the visions and actions of courageous women. Environmental movement like Chipko have become historical landmarks as they have been fuelled by the ecological insights and political and more strength of women (vandana shiva).

Chipko Movement was born in a small hilly village of Himalayas. The illiterate tribal women commenced this movement in December 1972. This movement became famous as the Chipko (which means to embrace) movement. The movement started in Tehri Garhwal district of Uttar Pradesh. It challenged the old belief that forests means only timber and emphasised their roles in making soil, water and pure air which are the basis of human life. This philosophy popularised the movement in many countries. The women of Advani village in Tehri Garhwal had tied the sacred thread around the trees, faced police firing in February 1978 and later courted arrest. This movement continued under the leadership of Sri Sunderlal Bahuguna in various villages.

The Chipko's plan is infact a slogan of planting five F's – Food, Fodder, Fuel, Fibre and Fertiliser on trees to make communities self sufficient in all their basic needs. It will protect environment and bring permanent peace, prosperity and happiness to mankind.

Chipko movement points out the links between women's burden as food providers and gatherers and their militancy in depending on natural resources and protecting them from violent devastation. The word "Chipko" originates from a particular form of non-violent action developed by hill women in the 19th century, fore runner of the recent movement.

Women's Non-violent Power in Chipko Movement

The Chipko movement against tree felling is a phenomenon of the last twenty years. On April 1974, the women of India's most poverty stricken district, Tehri-Garhwal whose annual per capita income was Rs.129/- rose against tree felling. It is being nationally and internationally discussed as the people's ecological movement for the protection of the natural environment. Since women are the gatherers of fuel, fodder and water, it is they who feel the first impact of soil erosion. Mindless destruction of the forests has seriously upset economy of the hill people . Men often migrate to the plains, women are left to cope with an ever more impoverished existence and to provide for the old and the children. Many women have been driven to suicide because of the increasing pressures on them. Therefore it is women who have seen through the government planning on which crores of rupees have been spent during the last 33 years. Women have repeatedly challenged administrators and politicians with their slogan "planning without fodder, fuel and water is one eyed planning". In the course of this movement, Garhwal women successfully undertook leadership roles and questioned the right of men to decide the fate of the forests or to enter into contractors without consulting the women, who would be the worst affected. The women said that "this forest is our home, we will not let it be cut down". The police force used all repressive and terrorising methods to retreat the non-violent strength of the women.

One of the woman called Gaura Devi led 27 village women to prevent the contractors employees and forest department personnel about 60 men in all, from going to the Reni forest to fell 2,415 trees. While the women were blocking the narrow passage leading to the forest, the men used all sorts of threats and later on the pretext of being drunk, even tried to misbehave with women. But the women refused to budge and bravely resisted all misbehaviour. One of the persons spat at Gaura Devi's face. The contractor tried to bribe Gaura Devi into letting his men enter the forest. When she refused this offer, the forest department personnel threatned to call the police and arrest her. Another instance of woman being harassed by the village men was in Dongri Paitoli village.

The Jungle is Our Parental Home

The slogan of the Chipko women is soil, water, vegetation are the gifts of the forest and are the basis of life. The fundamental tenet of ecology has not come to them from scientific research but has sprung from their daily experience and struggle to survive. These women knew that the commercialisation of the forest management means the erosion of the soil, which is the base of their existence and drying up of water sources.

TELANGANA MOVEMENT

The Telangana movement began in 1946 and continued till 1951. It is one of the two major post-war insurrectionary peasant struggles in India. The Telangana Movement (1946-51) was a protest of the people who wanted both food and freedom from the oppressive regime of the Nizam, the Patils and the Jagirdars in Hyderabad state. The basic feature of the life of people in Hyderabad state under the Nizam was the feudal exploitation that persisted till the uprising of the Telangana peasants. The peasants on the Nizam's personal estate were practically bonded to the ruler. Under the Jagirdari system various illegal taxes and forced labour were extracted from peasants by the landlords. Apart from this there were deshmukhs and despandes (principal revenue officers of a district who became land owners overtime) or tax collectors of the Nizam who grabbed thousands of acres of land and made it their own property. Peasants thus became tenants at will.

One common social phenomenon was the *vetti* system of forced labour and exactions imposed on all peasant sections in varying degrees. Each family had to send one person to collect wood for fuel, carry post to other villages, foot wear, agricultural implements, pots or cloth had to be supplied freely to landlords. Another system that prevailed was keeping of peasant girls as slaves in the landlords house. When the landlord's daughters were married these girls were often sent with them to serve as concubines.

When the exactions of the landlords reached the point of evicting peasants from their land, the peasants began to resist.

Sporadic struggles were launched in 1949 against the Deshmukhs of Visunur, Suryapet, Babasahebpet and Kalluru. The beginning of the Telangana peoples struggle in 1946 was against the Visunur Deshmuk when his hirelings murdered Doddi Kumarayya an Andhra Maha Sabha worker.

Large number of women who were desperate because of extreme poverty, slavery and sexual exploitation by the feudal lords had faught courageously in this movement. In order to mobilise and develop political consciousness among women, the communist party had formed a women's organisation which published a women's journal called *Andhra Vanitha*. Through this journal, they campaigned against child marriages and for widow remarriages and for increased wages and so on.

The conditions affecting the women of this time were doubly oppressive because of the additional burden they were forced to bear and crucially affected by the oppression of landlord and moneylender. Women who were a large section of the agricultural labour and tobacco leaf pickers, moved militantly into the struggle for land, better wages, fair rent, reasonable interest on cash and grain loans. They were subjected to *vetti* (compulsory services and exactions), bonded to the landlord, and exploited physically and sexually. Rape was an everyday reality, the undenied right of landlord or moneylender. *Adi bapa* or concubinage was prevalent. *Adi bapa* was a form of concubinage peculiar in Telangana, where a young girl usually from a bonded family had to accompany the bride to her husband's house to tend her mistress and to provide sexual service to the master. Her virginity was therefore as important as the bride's. The fact that girls had already been raped or seduced by a man in the house were attached to by birth often saved them from this fate.

The oppression of the upper class women was qualitatively different in the sense that the violence they faced was not visible and physical but invisible and structural. Purdah (seclusion) was strictly observed both by high caste Hindu and Muslim families. Child marriage and early widowhood were common. Education for women was unheard of. Outside the Nizam's state, social reform movements had already touched women's lives and the nationalist movement had brought women into public life. In Telangana the cultural dominance of Muslim feudal rule kept women out of the mainstream much longer. Fora, such as the Andhra Maha Sabha which sprang up to assert the cultural identity of the people, added women's education to their agenda of constitutional reform and civil liberties. Thus many women who were drawn into the cultural movements, drew closer to the Communist party which was working through the Andhra Maha Sabha. When the Andhra Maha Sabha added basic agrarian reforms to its programme of action these women also plunged into the struggle.

What was the response of women to the new horizons opening up before them? Suddenly, the four walls of the household seemed to fall apart and structures of feudal oppression, so unchanging and permanent in the past were not only being questioned but were also challenged in practice. A new socialist society was on the horizon. Women were being exhorted and required to come out and share the responsibility of building this new society where men and women would be equal. Paradoxically enough, although women are perceived as the guardians and preservers of traditional culture and although the very stability of any given society is perceived as resting on the purity and orthodoxy of its women. In practice women have achieved major gains during periods of war or revolution. It is only in such periods of social days-function, with the breakdown of constant surveillance and the mechanisms of discipline that normally objectify them, that women rush forth to grasp the opportunities for response and growth that become possible.

Let us see the life of women before the struggle. Sugunamma's first contact with the outside world occurred when her brother insisted her serving tea personally to their visitors. The brother also objected to his sister's marriage to an old, already married, rich man and tutored her to say no to the marriage. Listening to Sugunamma's account of how the whole village gathered to gasp at the unprecedented sight of a girl actually saying no, we learn how for a woman even the possibility of consent or choice in marriage was radical in its implications.

Lalitha, who was married at the age of five, after coming into the movement, when her husband was in jail, she went to her parents home to deliver a child. She had no choice but to subject herself to a purification ceremony where her "inner tongue" (uvula) was burnt with a hot golden wire. It is interesting how the punishment seeks to purity and discipline by fire her "inner tongue" for the abuse of her Brahmin taste through mixed eating (as a Brahmin she had lost her caste by eating with other castes). Lalitha shrugs off the physical pain of the incident but is evident that it has had the desired effect of searing her own humiliation and powerlessness into her memory. The punishment is also an example of how quickly deviant women can be reclaimed and disciplined by tradition at moments of physical helplessness.

The peasant women from Vempati in those days did not dare to wear a flower in their hair or to wear a good sari. It was not simply a question of seeming attractive and thus inviting sexual harassment. The harassment was already there. But the added fear of seeming to step beyond their station in life and the fear of what punishment it might bring was inhibiting enough.

Kamalamma's sister who came from a devadasi background escaped when she has been sent to an Adi bapa with the girl of the house since she seduced by one of the other men in the family. Koteshwaramma was married at the age of four and widowed at the age of five. When she was married again at eighteen, the groom came hiding in a heavily curtained cart, so that villagers would not attack her and prevent the marriage. Examples like these are abounded. Upper class women had to observe purdah in Telangana. Mallu Swarajyam describes how her mother could not be seen even by the washer woman except at a fixed hour on a fixed day. When bangle sellers came to the house the women thrust their hands out from under the curtain to have the bangles fitted. Dayani Kausalya tells us how they had never stepped out of the courtyard of the house into the fields before the struggle. Details such as these establish for the norms which circumscribed and defined women just a few years before the struggle but are so distanced from the present to belong, as it were, to another age. The changes that have come after the struggle are tangible and easy to see.

In most societies there has been a fairly clear demarcation of the public domain of war, production and politics and the private domain of the family, domestic labour, reproduction and sexuality. While men have moved fairly easily between the two women, by and large have been confined to the private domain. Peasant women have no doubt always had access into the public sphere of production but have remained at a level that is marginal and powerless. Further even the woman who is a wage labourer has with few exceptions internalised and accepted the sexual division of labour. They have always culturally and ideologically accepted the power and control of their men however powerless or oppressed the latter may be outside the home. From such a situation women were captulated, as it were, into a moment when everything entered the realm of possibility. They were asked to come and attend meetings. They were taught to read and write and discuss political questions. Political classes were held for them and they were told about their own country as well as about distant countries. The knowledge they gained as a result of these classes gave them the tools to understand their own social reality. For example, Kamalamma says "It was because of the Communist Party that my learning stood me in good stead and I knew at least this much. But my sister has just forgotten everything and it's all just wasted. The ideological framework provided by the Party helped the women to analyse their situation, process their knowledge and make sense of their surroundings". Priyamvada says, "It was the Party that made them human beings". Kondapalli Koteswaramma says, "It was the party that gave them the enthusiasm and said to come and join in struggle". Peasant women like Salamma said "One should work in the Sangham and die. One should be born to live with strength, the strength is our shoulders. How did my wisdom grow out of this?..... I sued to graze buffaloes but its all at the tip of my tongue..... The struggle for gruel and water—I lived in such strength and power for it". The opportunity to act, the power to fight for control over their own lives gave the women an identity, a sense of enormous strength and wisdom. Chakali Ailamma, a figure of significance because one of the earliest struggles was for her land says "my husband was nobody, my sons, they are nobody. Wherever you go, whatever you do it is my name they will mention first ... you must be like Ailamma they say". All the women refer to the party or the Sangham as the basis and the cause of their liberation.

Koteshwaramma describes her fear of marrying again, afraid that her ill luck would kill the man who married her. She also spoke of the support and encouragement of the men in the party. Later she went on stage, acting and singing as part of the cultural squad of the party. She talks of her misgivings and anxiety when she had to go on stage. She explains that it was the assurance that the Party would protect the women who acted that finally gave them the confidence. Respectable women did not act in those days. Crossing the barrier of respectability, although eventually liberating in its effect is painful and frightening for women initially.

As the women became active in the Sanghams they were asked to take up issues specific to women and organise the peasant women around these issues. Two different reasons emerge for the mobilisation of women from the accounts of the women themselves. Manikonda Suryavathi says "the members of the Sanghams sent their wives and sisters to the classes. They believed that if men were to be emancipated, if they were to become highly conscious then the consciousness should also spread to the home. This was elementary to their education". She also said that, when the educated women formed clubs, they did not allow ordinary women to join. And so they wanted to start Sanghams for women who were peasants or agricultural labourers.

Thus there was a deliberate attempt to mobilise women and to take up campaigns that would affect their practical interest. Priyamvada says how the discussions included issues like wages, wife beating, child care, hygiene and the right to breast feed infants during work. Both Suryavathi and Udayam explained of a campaign called "model housewife", "where the women were taught to cook nutritious food, bring up healthy infants, keep their environment clean and which also included conducting various sports and games for women. One campaign in Andhra Pradesh which was extremely popular was constructing toilets for women. The Navjivan Mahila Mandal situated in Hyderabad, took up the distribution of ration cards, cheap grain coupons and maintaining milk centers. The women who came to these centers were eventually politicised to oppose the atrocities of the Razakars. PramilaTaj's work in the Navjivan Mahila Mandal gave her such a network of sympathetic contacts that she was able to arrange for the shelter and the support of many underground party comrades during periods of acute repression. Both the Navjivan Mahila Mandal and the Mahila Sanghams (Women's organisations) were successful in reaching out to women because they took up issues of practical gender interests to women i.e., issues arising from their concrete conditions of existence and women's specific place in the existing division of labour. One of the reasons the party found it necessary to mobilise women was also because it would be easier to get support during periods of repression. But while such problems were taken up in an attempt to involve women, we do not find that there was an awareness of these gender specific areas as valid sites of political struggle. We find that although the interest of women in such issues arose from their subordination, mobilisation around these issues drew their loyalty and support without leading to an increased awareness of the nature or source of that subordination.

The peasant women who formed the backbone of the resistance undoubtedly came into the struggle for land, for better wages, abolition of *vetti* and against exorbitant interest on grain and cash loans. In the thick of the struggle and bearing the brunt of repression their interests were bound to the cause in a way which made their participation inevitable. Accounts tell us how two hundred peasant women stood together in Penukonda and chased the police out of the village. In Appajipet, women encircled a police van, attacked the police with pestles and chilli powder and secured the release of their Sangham activists. Women from villages like Akkirajupalli were constantly beaten, tortured and raped by Razakars in an attempt to crush the resistance. They refused to reveal the where abouts of the Sangham activists in spite of severe torture. Gajjela Ballamma of Akkirajupalli says my husband was also in the Party that's why the Razakars were so furious. The whole of Akkirajupalli became famous.

Vajramma describes "In those days when the Razakars asked to dance Bathakamma (dance performed at the festival of Bathakamma, a local mother goddess) they have danced. They stripped when they asked to strip. But for their staunch support and commitment the movement could not have survived for nearly six years. In dire want themselves, they shared the little food they had with the Sangham activists. Fully aware that supplying food and shelter would bring more repression they evolved their own system of passing messages and relaying food to the squads in the forests.

Rape was an every day reality, the underlined right of landlord or moneylender or Adi bapa. Concubinage was prevalent. Adi bapa was a form of concubinage peculiar to Telangana, where a young girl usually from a bonded family had to accompany the bride to her husbands house to tend her mistress and to provide sexual service to the master. The oppression of the upper class women was qualitatively different in the sense that the violence they faced was not visible and structural purdah was strictly observed both by high caste Hindu and Muslim women. Child marriage and early widowhood were common. Education for women was unheard of outside the Nizam's state social reform movements had already touched women's lives and the nationalist movement had brought women into public life. In Telangana the cultural dominance of Muslim feudal rule kept women out of the mainstream much longer. Andhra Maha Sabha, which sprang up to assert the cultural identity of the people added women's education to their agenda of constitutional reform and civil liberties. Thus many women who were drawn into the cultural movements, drew closer to the communist party which was working through the Andhra Maha Sabha. When the Andhra Maha Sabha added basic agrarian reforms to its programme of action, these women also plunged into the struggle.

Women from all classes drawn into the movement not only responded with energy and commitment but moved with a new found deliberate skill both into the urban middle class as well as into the peasant sections of the population drawing their support slowly but surely into the movement. The communist party which seriously took up issues of social reforms for women like widow remarriage, prohibition of child marriage, education for women and better opportunities also began to identify women of ability and drew them into the movement. Some of the women who took active role and participation in the movement were Dudala Salamma, Kamalamma, Regalla Achamamba, Chityala Ailamma, Peasaru Satbamma, Kondapalli Koteshwaramma, Mallu Swarajyam, Dayani Kausalya, PramilaTai, Chakilam Lalithamma, Bullemma, Narasamma, Vijramma, Subbamma, Sugunamma etc.

The Communist Party in Andhra served as a rear base for the Telangana struggle arranging for relief and supplies and keeping in touch with the struggle areas. The entry of the Indian Army into Hyderabd in September the police action as it was called brought the surrender of the Nizam and the disbanding of the Razakars. The force of the Army was now turned on the peasants and the Communist Party was banned and repression increased. The rich peasantry withdrew its support once the Nizam was gone and the squads had to retreat into the forests. Finally the struggle was withdrawn in 1951.

In 1951, when the movement was withdrawn some changes were took place. Forced labour was abolished, village committees continued to be active and people resisted the return of the old Jagirdari system. The demand for division along linguistic zones to facilitate all round political, social and cultural development of the people was also subsequently pushed forward. More important was the fact that it had set a revolutionary tradition among the Telugu people.

SRIKAKULAM MOVEMENT

In post-Independence, Srikakulam period was the first district in Andhra Pradesh to witness an armed struggle led by the Marxist-Leninist variant of the Communist Party of India.

It was brutal and brief and by 1970, it had been crushed. A significant feature of this movement was the participation of women in unprecedented numbers and the impact it had on their consciousness.

The Srikakulam district is topographically divided into two regions, the agency areas which are hilly, mainly inhabited by tribals, and the plains and coastal areas. It was in the former that the movement was more intense and had a much greater participation of women. The movement started in 1960 when there was an armed uprising in that area by an organisation of tribals called 'Girijan Sangham', it was on the issues of land and wages and against the nexus between the exploitative landlords, moneylenders, forest revenue officials and the police.

The Srikakulam movement was essentially the struggle of the Girijans for justice and for fair play. It started with meetings of peasants. The landlords took the offensive and fired upon their procession at Mondekallu and it was a signal for the movement. It was of three stages. In the first stage guerilla bands took to action against landlords. In the second stage the people were called upon to take advantage of the action against the landlords. Promisory notes were torn and debt bonds were burnt. Pledged gold and silver articles were returned to mortagagors. Naturally the people responded. In the third stage the people themselves took part in the raids against the landlords. Thus in the second and third stages of the movement the women too played their role. They did not lag behind. They did not betray their leaders even when they were subjected to torture. Girijan women were put in jail in considerable number.

Women of that region helped the guerilla bands. They acted as couriers and watch and ward staff. Some enterprising women joined guerilla bands and lost their lives at the hands of the police. Panchadri Nirmala aged 22 was the mother of two children. She joined the movement alongwith her husband. Her husband was killed by the landlords, and the police. She filled his place in the guerilla group. She avenged her husband's death. She participated in the annihilation of class enemies. She was caught when the police rapped her guerilla group. She was shot dead by the police.

Bommareddi Snehalatha was another memorable woman. A girl in her teens, she left her parental home and fled to the jungle. In those days jungle is a bye-word for revolt on Naxalberi of variety. She died as a victim of the police "encounter".

The women followed the leadership of men in several movements. They spared no effort in their endeavour. They proved themselves equal to men in respect of courage, determination and suffering but still they were not allowed to take an important role in decision-making.

ANTI-RAPE MOVEMENT

Political Background of the Anti-Rape Movement

With the declaration of emergency, many of the activities got dampened as a result of heavy repression. Even women's groups and organisations engaged in protest-movements had to bear the brunt of emergency rule. Anti-Price-Rise, Women's Organisations (Bombay and Baroda), Progressive Organisation of Women (Hyderabad), and Women's Groups in Bihar were badly affected by the emergency rule. Women's organisations with massive membership who resorted to direct action had to face repression and their activities came to a halt. However for observing International Women's Year, many activities like holding seminars or organising committees, passing resolutions, publishing papers etc., highlighting women's position got state patronage. Mass media, policy makers, academicians and general population became aware of the problems of women and a new consciousness and alertness to women's issues was generated.

When the emergency period was over, issues of Civil Liberties were hotly debated. Repression of political activists and political prisoners by the state, highlighted by the mass media generated. Instances of mass rapes of poor, Dalit and tribal women in Madhya Pradesh, Bihar, Rajasthan, Uttar Pradesh and Maharashtra appeared in the newspapers. Rape was discussed as an issue of civil liberty. Awareness about democratic rights brought with its awareness about atrocities on women.

Organisations like Mahila Dakshita Samiti, Samta Manch and Stree Sangharsh Samiti were formed in Delhi. In Bombay, women's groups like Stree Mukti Sangathana, Socialist Women's Group, Feminist Network Collective (FNC) came into existence. Purogami Sangathana (Pune), Stree Shakti Sangathana (Hyderabad), and Pennurimai Iyyakum (Madras) are also autonomous women's organisations which came into existence in the post-emergency period. Moreover in Kanpur, Patna, Kolhapur, Madras, Aurangabad, Raipur and other smaller cities also autonomous women's groups started blooming. Pune women's liberationists started a bi-monthly called Baija (rural women) in Marathi. In 1978, when the socialist women's group of feminists organised a workshop of women activists in Bombay many thought provoking papers were presented. After three days of rigorous debate, it was decided to form a coordination committee of women activists working in various parts of the country to start a newsletter in English and Hindi called *Feminist Network* and *Stree Sangharsh* respectively and to publish a women's magazine in Hindi and English called *Manushi*. During 1978-79, six (6) issues of *Feminist Network* were published. This newsletter got very good feed-back from women's groups and organisations all over India. In January 1979, when the first issue of *Manushi* was published many feminists felt that to sustain *Manushi* they would put all their energy to it because it was a big venture and to sustain a non-commercial feminist journal required abundant resources. *Manushi* was treated as a mouthpiece for autonomous women's movement in the country and also seen as a product of collective efforts by the feminists. At this stage, differences of analytical framework to understand the problems of women started coming to the fore. Those who merely wanted to make some minor reforms in the existing social structure and remain contented with some liberal statutory measures came to be known as "Bourgeoisie Feminists". Those who found men only (to be specific "Power relations between men and women" only), responsible for the miseries of women are known as "Radical Feminists". And those who admit role of patriarchy in subjugating women in our society but at the same time believe that in this system other oppressed and exploited masses like dalits, tribals, working class are also allies of women's liberation movement and that is why, believe in solidarity with these strata are known as "Socialist Feminists". In the context of *Manushi* sharp discussions took place on the various trends among the Feminists.

The gang-rape by police on a beggar woman called Laxmi in Punjab and Rameezabee and Shakeelabee in Hyderabad raised public fury, because civil liberties organisations took up these cases. Democratic Rights organisations and bold journalists also brought into light the cases of mass-rapes in Pantnagar, Rajhara, Goa, Singhbhum, Marathwada, Agra, Bhojpur, Karimnagar and North-eastern states. It was in this background that the famous Mathura rape case came to light and sparked off the anti-rape movement throughout the country. By the end of 1979, when four professors from Delhi University wrote an open letter to the judge of the Supreme Court of India condemning the judgement on the Mathura rape case, organisations all over the country came out in the streets demanding the reopening of the Mathura rape case as well as called for amendments in the existing rape law.

A 14-year old girl, Mathur was summoned to the Police Station late in the night at Chandrapur, a small town near Nagpur. Two police constables raped her. The Sessions Court of Nagpur alleged Mathura to be of loose morals and declared the policemen-rapists innocent. The High Court convicted the rapists and lashed seven and half years rigorous imprisonment. But the Supreme Court reversed the decision and alleged that Mathura had given consent to sexual intercourse with the policemen. This blatant anti-woman judgement gave birth to nation-wide anti-rape protests. From every corner of the country, women's groups strongly demanded reopening of the Mathura case and at the same time demanded amendments in the rape law. Demonstrations and meetings were organised everywhere. In this movement autonomous organisations of women had taken initiative. Many rallies were organised all over the country on 8th March 1980. The Government was pressurised by hot debates in newspapers, magazines and through signature campaigns, slogans, and posters. During this period anti-rape organisations and women's organisations were set up in various cities. Political parties which initially did not take up this problem seriously started issuing statements and calling public meetings and rallies on this question after March 1980. At the time of the Maya Tyagi rape case, all opposition parties started shouting about "deteriorating law and order situation". In the winter session of the Parliament, Government declared its intention to introduce a bill relating to rape and presented a draft. Women's organisations, political parties and sensitive people started discussing different aspects of this bill. Never since independence people had shown such consciousness against police excesses.

The Government had to accept the demand of women's organisations to re-open the Mathura rape case. Thus, a situation was created wherein political parties could not easily be indifferent to this strong current of autonomous women's organisations.

The Forum Against Rape (now, Forum Against Oppression of Women) in Bombay and Forum Against Rape in Nagpur had also taken up individual cases of women's oppression. The organisation in Bombay did active work on issues like dowry, rape, wife beating etc. In Kanpur, Patna, Ahmedabad, Baroda, Raipur, Pune, Calcutta, Madurai, Arkonam, Delhi, Hyderabad, Madras and Bangalore such groups came into existence. These organisations attracted lawyers, doctors, professors, students and working women in particular. This nation-wide movement enhanced the awareness towards women's problems. All parties started strengthening the women's wing by paying more attention towards its development.

Issue Based Movements in India Since 1970's

The movements against several social evils concerning women were organised by several male crusaders who were also important leaders of the nationalist movement. Women participated under their leadership in the struggle against social evils and also for national independence. With the achievement of national independence major agitational activities were withdrawn.

The important characteristics of the III phase of women's movement i.e. from post independence era to 1985 are as follows: till the 1970's a kind of passivity or accommodation due to the socio-economic circumstances of free India influenced the women's movement. Where the economic crisis of 1960's created an atmosphere in which issues concerning women are more and in which women started taking part. The period from 1976-1985 (International women's decade) saw the emergence of autonomous women's movement in which autonomous women's groups and organisations started movements for liberation.

Ideals of equal status for women and important provision for the welfare of women were incorporated into the Indian Constitution, while the pre-independent legislative acts continued to be in force. The Constitution guaranteed equal rights to both the sexes. Article 15 and Article 16 (2) of the Constitution forbids discrimination are accepted as being equal in the eyes of the law (Article 14) and the franchise is granted to men and women above 21 years of age. In the early 1950's a series of legislations such as the Hindu Marriage Act, Hindu Succession Act, Dowry Prohibition Act and Equal Remuneration Act were passed.

The emergence of independent India as a welfare state also affected the contours of Indian women's movement. The Government had started a Central Social Welfare Board (CSWB) to promote welfare and development services for women, children and under privileged sections of the society. It has a nation-wide programme for grants-in-aid for welfare activities with a special emphasis on women's welfare.

The period from the late 1960's has been marked by economic crisis and stagnation, rising prices, increasing landlessness and generalised discontent both in the rural and urban areas. The left parties took interest in the economic crisis and started organising movements. Through women's issues were not taken up, women were mobilised in large number and they participated in the general struggle of the rural poor, tribals and industrial working class. Women's organisations such as Shramik Mahila Sangathana (the working women's organisation) took up the issue of rising prices of essential goods, adulteration etc.

The anti price-rise movement of 1973 was organised by united front organisation of women belonging to political parties such as CPI (M), Socialist Party Congress and even non-political house wives. The political parties felt the need to mobilise women to achieve their own political gains. This resulted in the establishment of National Federation of Indian women (NFIW) by Communist Party of India. The economic hardships of the rural masses have also drawn the attention of some political parties. While pressing for better working conditions for peasant women, issues like wife beating, alcoholism, dowry and sexual harassment from the upper castes were also given attention. Thus in the early 1970's though women's organisations were carrying programmes of cultural activities, craft classes, beauty shows, the poor women were getting entrenched into the wider movements. The left political parties in their mass movements were mobilising women and at certain points of time, women took the leadership and along with other demands focussed attention on women's issues, the best example is the Chipko movement for ecological conservation.

Paying unequal wages to women for equal work is a part of the general discrimination against women in the work place especially in the agriculture, plantations, mines and other unorganised industries. Working women's hostels, crèches, legal facilities and trade union rights were not available to women. Mortality rate among women was higher than that of men due to malnutrition. Violence against women appears in the form of dowry deaths, wife battering, mass rape during caste and communal riots, gang rape, sexual harassment of women and indecent representation of women in media, poverty and deprivation affect the condition of Dalit and tribal women. Many of were are forced to prostitution. Caste and communal riots make the conditions of these women the worst.

Autonomous women's movements emerged during the international women's decade. The decade not only provided an opportunity for drawing the attention to women's issues but it also stimulated the growth of new women's groups. During the year 1975, 8th March was celebrated as a international women's day. Important features of the women's autonomous movements were that women organised themselves and led the movement. The women's organisations started fighting against oppression, exploitation, injustice and discrimination and this movement was not subordinated to the decisions and necessities of the political or social groups organisations.

The women's organisations that emerged during the autonomous movement period could be divided into the following six categories:

- Autonomous groups whose nature is mainly agitational, propagandism and consciousness raising;
- Grassroot or mass based organisations like trade unions, agricultural labourers organisations, democratic groups, tribal organizations etc in which women's issues like wife beating, sexual harassment by the landlords, alcoholism of men have been taken up;
- Groups that concentrate on providing services, shelter homes etc to the needy women;
- Professional women's organisations such as doctors, lawyers etc that seek to agitate against discrimination more often create alternate channels for professional activity;
- Women's wings or fronts of the political parties;
- Groups involved in research and documentation on women's issues.

The above mentioned groups and organisations take up women's problems and its members are only women and they are run by women without any interference from any party. They have interesting names which highlight feminine solidarity and women power namely *Saheli* (female friend), *Manushi* (woman) *Stri Shakti, Nari Samata Manch* etc. *Mahila Dakshita Samiti, Sangarsh Samiti in Delhi, Stri Mukti Sangathana, Socialist women's group* in Bombay, *Purogami Sanghatana* in Pune, *Stree Shakti Sanghatana* in Hyderabad, *Pennurimai Iyyakam* in Madras are the various women's organisations that came into existence. All these groups have taken up various issues like atrocities against women, rape, alcoholism, wife beating, dowry harassment and murder, violence in the family, problems of working women, oppression of lower class, caste and minority women, media distortion of women's image, personal laws, health issues, problems of women in slums etc. They issued pamphlets, collected signatures to support their demand, organised and protest rallies and demonstrations to mobilise public opinion etc. They also organised street corner meetings, street plays, skits and songs and poster exhibitions. Many feminist magazines are being published for e.g. Manushi, Saheli etc.

The autonomous movement besides creating general awareness on women also exposed the judiciary as in the Mathura rape case, in removing the bill boards which showed obscene scenes or stopping shows or plays where women were treated as sex symbols. Autonomous movement has also given rise to special interest groups involved in the anti-dowry and anti-rape campaigns. More research is being carried out on subjects related to women. In the academic field women's studies are taken more seriously. As a result of the pressure created by the women's movement amendments in the laws regarding rape, dowry, marriage, Prevention of Women for Domestic Violence Act 2005 are made.

ANTI-ARRACK MOVEMENT

The anti-arrack movement of women in Andhra Pradesh was one of the most historic and significant movements of the decade of 1990's. The historic battle waged by the women in Andhra Pradesh against the social evil of alcohol drinking is a magnum war in Indian social history. Women have played a historic role in bringing about a ban on consumption and sale of distilled liquor in Andhra Pradesh. The movement indeed was not just for elimination of liquor but for the protection and survival of their own culture. The rural women in the villages raised their voices lifted their hand to arrest the degeneration of the progress of their families and the damage caused by their men to their children and themselves.

The movement was started in a small village called "Dubagunta" in Nellore district of Andhra Pradesh. The main reason for the movement was said to be the successful literacy mission that was going on in Nellore district. In one of the adult education classes under the National Literacy Mission (NLM), the story of Seethamma was narrated to a group of men and women. In that story an agricultural labourer called Seethamma, recognising the destruction being caused to her neighbour's families by the arrack addicted husband, gathered all the women, launched an agitation and succeeded in closing down the only arrack shop in the village.

Seethamma story, a lesson in adult literacy classes was the main inspiration for the women. To them, Seethamma was not just a character in the story but a model to emulate. If she, as an agricultural labourer could launch an agitation single handedly they too could do so. A few weeks later three men of their village who were drunk fell into a well accidently and died. This accident spurred the opportunity to identify the liquor as the root cause of all their miseries and the women in Nellore district raised slogans, such as "give up drink and wakeup from ignorance", "gave up drink and protect health" etc. Rosamma led the women of Dubagunta Village in Nellore district which started the anti arrack movement in Andhra Pradesh in the year 1992.

Other villages followed suit. The village women of Nellore district learnt the art of cooperating with others. Struggle taught them new lessons. In the fight they stood shoulder to shoulder. They defied the excise authorities, the police who rushed to protect the liquor traders and lastly the goondas and hirelings of the liquor contractors. They could enforce complete boycott of liquor in their villages. They heard that the excise authorities intend to conduct sales of liquor licences. Naturally they became agitated. The social workers, women and men stood by them. The voluntary agencies working in the districts lent them support. The workers of several political parties came to their aid let they lose their popularity. The opposition parties thought in fit to aid and strengthen the women's struggle. Thirty thousand women (3000) assembled at Nellore to thwart the sales of liquor licences. They faced threats, braved lathis, heat and cold and stood steadfast in their determination to stop the sales. Thirty-two times they could stop the sales in Nellore district.

The women's movement of Nellore inspired the women of the other districts of Andhra Pradesh. They too took up the struggle. It became a mighty movement with the support of men of voluntary agencies and the political parties.

Anti-arrack movement was a spontaneous outburst of poor, lower class and lower caste women who just learnt what 'literacy'. The unity and the collective strength shown by the women in Andhra Pradesh cut across caste and class barriers for the first time. Women's frustration and anger suddenly burst out into a spontaneous protest against the local arrack shops, the excise officials, the liquor contractors and all the machineries of state involved in the trade.

The anti-arrack agitation took different forms viz. peaceful and violent. The peaceful agitators barred entry of arrack into villages, prevented sale of liquor and went to the extent of putting the drunkards to shame by social boycott and disgracing them some times. Other agitators not so about means broke up the liquor shops, illicit distilleries and beat up the drunkards. They destroyed barrels of liquor sought to be brought into the licenced shops. Police rushed to the aid of liquor contractors and it is reported that nearly 1706 cases were registered against the agitators both, men and women.

Apart from preventing the local liquor shops from functioning by destroying arrack, burning sachets and forcing local sellers to close their shops, the women have resisted their pressure tactics and attacks from contractors, excise department officials and the excise police. The inspirational guidance extended by the veteran freedom fighter Mr. Vavilala Gopala Krishnaiah, added momentum to the movement organised by the rural women. Within a few days the struggle spread to all villages in the district. Soon all the arrack supply sources were blocked. There were spontaneous and simultaneous demonstrations in all the areas against the evils of arrack consumption.

In continuation of the agitation some women went on rampage cutting the palm trees and not allowing the authorities to reach the venue of the auctions. Nellore district collector tried to pacify women agitators introduced tickets to auction bidders and also promised them that in future the arrack business will be confined to professionals only. Not satisfied with this action, the women agitators forced the auctions to be put off indefinitely. The arrack dealers were in trouble. They could neither sell their liquor nor protect it from the agitators.

The opposition parties supported the women's anti-arrack agitation. The Communist parties – CPI, CPI (M) and CPI (ML) – contributed their mite to the spread and strength of the agitation. Coordination committees at district levels with men and women supporting the same came into existence. At the State level there arose an 'Anti-Arrack Women's Struggle Committee' with representatives of women's associations with opposition party orientation and unattached women leaders.

The women's struggle in Andhra Pradesh consisted of 20 non-political organisations who came together to fight for the scaping of auctions and to bring about a complete ban on future manufacture and sale of arrack. All these organisations came under a single umbrella to form the A.P. Anti-arrack struggle committee with Ms. Renuka Chowdary as the chairperson.

The noteworthy feature of women's movement is that it based on the Gandhian principles. In support of the movement, various co-operative societies in the state have declared that in future loan facilities would be extended only to those who give up drinking.

The anti-arrack (distilled liquor) agitation launched by women of Andhra Pradesh in 1992 and 1993 was crowned with success when the Chief Minister of the State announced a policy of prohibition of sale of arrack immediately in Nellore District from 1st October 1993 in the entire State. It has carved out for itself a glorious chapter in the history of Women's Movement.

The agitation of Andhra Pradesh inspired people of other States and especially Haryana to take up similar campaigns. It is noted for the following factors:

- Several sections of the people took part and supported it;
- Women of all classes took the initiative;
- The opposition parties to lent their support to the cause;
- The government was forced to bow down to the wishes of the people;
- The women realized their strength and importance;
- The women drew lessons from their miserable lives as inmates of families of drunkards;
- The women became self-reliant to a large extent;
- The women of all political learnings strove their utmost to make the agitation a success. The battle is not completely won as toddy from palmyrah trees and IMFL (Indian made foreign liquor) are still allowed to be sold by the Government of the State.

It is not out of place to delineate the course of the agitation and struggle. The anti-arrack agitation had a small beginning at the out set. Several factors contributed to its rise. The literacy programme launched by the Government of State of A.P. was seized by several voluntary agencies as a golden opportunity to spread enlightenment among the people. A lesson in a literacy text book awakened the women to the evils of alcoholism. By that time they realised the intensity of their sufferings, physical, economic, and psychological. They also suffered due to lack of nutritious food, loss of self-respect and inability to bear the burden of the family. They thought that they came to a breaking point. They could not bear their hardships any more. They came to the conclusion that they must find a way out. They pondered over their situation. They identified the arrack traders, retail and wholesale as their enemies. They detested the excise authorities for giving protection to the liquor vendors. They thought it best to deny opportunities to men to purchase and consume liquor by getting the liquor shops closed and stop the sales of liquor licences.

The movement of women has to be looked at as the fall out of government policies. The cuts in the items of budgets—Central and state—in respect of social welfare programmes and the gathering of money by the state on account of liquor trade at the expense of the people and to their detriment have aggravated the situation. In a way the movement is a protest against Government policies and programmes. Finally, anti-arrack agitation has to be looked at from the feminist point of view. The women of A.P. could no longer bear the insults and humiliation caused by the consumption of liquor by their men. They took it up as a means for assertion of their identity and their right to peaceful family life and equal partnership in home. Though they have not articulated their views so explicitly, their protest was not only against liquor but against the male-domination. They refused to be treated as unequal and as sex-objects by men. It was indeed a great social experiment.

Women's Movements Between Developed and Developing Countries

Developed countries with a high degree of industrialisation, greater participation of women in employment and activities outside home are on a different footing compared to most developing countries with an agrarian structure, relatively low levels of women's participation in employment outside the home. Generally speaking, the former is likely to have the higher levels of gender equality. Compared to the latter which ought to have relatively higher levels of gender equality. Given the broad scenario, the problems women encounter, the issues they take up in the movement for equality or emancipation are likely to differ from one another. Issues apart, the socio-economic and political environments do condition the nature of women's movement as well as the degree of their participation.

Before making a comparison of women's movement in developed and developing countries, in terms of commonalties and differences in the nature of issues, a broad understanding of the movements in these countries is essential. Keeping this in view an attempt is being made first to present the women's movement in USA representing the developed countries and Sri Lanka, Africa and Latin American countries.

Women's Movement in USA

Women's movement in USA can be considered as a trendsetter for similar movements in different parts of the globe, particularly feminist movements in the 20th century. This provides a strong cause for choosing USA to represent the developed countries.

Broadly, women's movement in USA can be considered under two phases, the first up to 1920, when women gained the vote. It is then that women felt that they have achieved independence completely. The second phase started with the emergence of feminist movement in 1960 onwards after a standstill of 40 years.

Women's Movement in USA up to 1920

Women's movements in USA originated in their quest for equality with men. The earliest attempt in this direction was made by challenging the Puritan theocracy of Boston by Anne Hutchinson, for denying voice to women in church affairs. During the colonial period, women agitated against high prices of British Tea and organised anti-tea leagues in New England and Middle Atlantic States.

During the war of Independence, when men are absent serving the continental armies, women played an active part in supply of clothes to the army, foreshadowing the famous sanitary commission of the civil war fame and later the Red Cross.

Women's movement as an organised one took shape only after the independence during the 19th century. The first attempt was a demand for educational facilities for women by Emma Williard in early 1820's. As a result Oberlin became the first college to open its doors for both men and women in 1833. Around the same time, the movement for abolition of slavery gave a political impetus to women's rights. Women's delegation from USA participated in the worldwide anti-slavery convention held at London in 1840. After their return from England, Molt and Stanton pressed for reforms on the issue of women's property and family rights. In the women's rights convention held at Seneca, popularly known as the Seneca Falls Convention held during the 19th and 20th July 1848. 300 men and women approved the Declaration of sentiments modeled on the Declaration of Independence. The prominent demands of the women at this convention related to control over property and earnings, guardianship of the children and right to divorce etc.

From 1848 to the beginning of Civil War such conventions of women's rights were held almost every year in different cities. After the 13th Amendment abolished slavery, they focussed attention towards suffrage through lecture tours, lobbying activities and petition campaigns etc. But in 1890 the National Women's Suffrage Association was formed by merging the earlier two associations i.e., American Women's Suffrage Association. Under the leadership of Alice Paul, a young and extremely militant suffragist, women organised parades, mass demonstrations, hunger strikes courted arrest till they succeeded in forcing the congress to ratify the women's suffrage amendment on 26th August 1920. With the passage of this amendment both public as well as women felt that they gained complete equality.

Forces of Change

Since 1920, many changes have taken place in the United States having an impact on women. The expanding frontiers of the United States helped to create a vague feminist bias. The Industrial Revolution provided them opportunities to follow men out of the home. It also influenced the rural and urban women towards the feminist movement.

Women's Movement in USA Since1960's

The report of the President's Commission on Status of Women in 1963 was made on the widespread discrimination in the pay on the basis of sex, despite equal pay laws in effect in 22 states. It also reported on barriers for employment and promotion to higher level posts in administration. This discrimination is more manifest in respect of Negro women due to race inadequate education and training. This discontentment coupled with the double burden of employment and housework made them restless. This sowed seeds of women's liberation movement and the cult of 'New Feminism'.

New Feminism

Diverse groups with varied demands are involved in the women's lib movement. Some focussing attention on personality development and some other on their marginalisation in the labour force. However, to most women of the lib movement new feminism means "rejecting the Barbie-doll stereotypical model of women as staple–navel playmate or smiling airline stewardess". In brief it includes equality with men on all fronts.

American feminists opposed the use of Mrs. and Miss that reveals their marital status. They have invented a new word called "MS" who became a symbol as well as a fad. The "New feminists" stress that women should take up housework by her choice rather than on consideration of tradition or on man's insistence.

The "new feminists" have emphasised that if women have to assume the roles of housekeeper, wife, mother and family representative in the community, it should be on her choice rather than from tradition or on man's insistence.

The major areas of concern for "New Feminism" in America are firstly they insist that there are no inherent emotional, intellectual or psychological difference between men and women. All differences are rooted in nature and a reflection of the socially imposed values.

Secondly they look at social values that distinguish male and female as a system of sex-role stereotypes. Basically the women's movement has been a middle-class one attracting the educated and relatively affluent into its fold. Joan D. Mandle, a Sociologist has distinguished between these broad groupings within the American feminist movement.

The first group represents those concerned with societal limits to their personal development and personal fulfillment. Young collegiate educated women who largely constitute this group often recognise and expose the contradictions between a culture that emphasise equality, opportunity and individual development and a social structure which tends a woman towards stereotyped low status roles. This group demands far radical change in the socialisation and development process to which both young women and men are exposed.

The second group largely representing the employed women are concerned about discrimination in work and occupation based on sex stereotypes. Their demands center on equal pay, security and an end to all forms of discrimination against women workers.

For the third group issues like organisation of family life, child bearing and domestic care are more salient. While some among this group call for an end to the social institution of family altogether, others call for reduced weekly work for both men and women and adoption of identical roles for both father and mother.

Despite its growing prominent in the recent past, many in the U.S., still characterise the entire movement and its goals as 'Utopian'. They argue "true equality between autonomous partners is hard to achieve even if both partners are of the same sex. The careful balancing of roles and obligations and privileges without the traditional patterns to fall back upon, sometimes seem like an almost-Utopian vision".

Women's Movement in Sri Lanka

Women's participation in social, economic and political movement in Sri Lanka despite high levels of women's literacy, greater participation in outside employment, particularly plantations appears to be rather limited. Many factors account for lack of significant women's movement in Sri Lanka.

The process of "Westernisation" which was the emergence of a Sri Lankan society which functioned in terms of standards, values and characteristics of Western Society caused a significant transformation in the position of Sri Lankan women. Sri Lanka had a long tradition of providing social security and social benefits for it citizens.

The Sri Lankan Constitution ideologically commits the nation to the realisation of equal rights for women. Unlike other developing countries, neither the predominant religion nor the colonial traditions pose ideological constraints on the articulation of equal rights.

The women who are successful in national politics have had either the capacity or the motivation to improve the situation facing other women. In fact, they preached women to accept women's traditional roles as mother and housewife. The speech delivered by Mrs. Bandarnaike in connection with International Women's year in 1975 testified the above views. She said "Women have a great responsibility in strengthening world peace and ushering in its prosperity. One way of achieving this is through the performance of onerous and vast responsible duty of caring for their families and bringing up their children to be good citizens. The other is by guiding the future generations in the proper path and inculcating correct ways of thinking in them, thus paving the way not only for personal and social upliftment of all humanity. It is my firm belief that we should make it a point not to forget the very important place of women who are occupying an important place in family life and in bringing up their children properly" (Kamala Wathie, 1990).

The above factors perhaps account for the absence of any significant women's movement in Sri Lanka, despise hardship women of encounter in family and work place.

Kumudhini Rose in her article on "Organising Women Workers in the Free Trade Zone, Sri Lanka", points out, though Sri Lanka has a rich heritage of organised trade union movement since independence in 1948, men continue to dominate and structure it according to their particular demands. Workers irrespective of sex are mobilised around general working class demands. Women are denied leadership levels of the trade unions but also that their specific problems have rarely been taken up within the movement. When the issue of women's oppression was raised in Sri Lanka in 1975 during the UN decade for women, it was considered as unimportant and secondary and considered to be dividing the working class movement. She also reflected on the reasons for lack of unionisation the labour force of 27,000 workers in the Free Trade Zone of which 85 per cent are women.

Political Participation of Women in Sri Lanka

The first political initiative of Sri Lankan women on their own was in 1925 when the specific issue of women's rights granting of limited rights for women of the country was proposed by Mallika Kulangana Samithiya at the General Assembly of the Ceylon National Congress. In 1927, women in the Ceylon National Congress viz., Mrs. George E. De Silva, Mrs. E.R. Thamikutty and Lady Solomon Dias, Bandarnaike formed a women Franchise Union and presented evidence before the Donaghmere Commission. Though Sri Lankan women obtained the right to vote in 1931, achievements in legal rights and a progressive narrowing of sex differences in education and literacy confirmed to the worldwide pattern of limited political participation by women. Kamala Wathie observed "In running for public office, notwithstanding the constitutional imperative for equality and despite having the world's first woman Prime Minister (1960) Sri Lankan women have played a very limited role. For over the decades in every Parliament women members are less than four per cent, though they form nearly half of the adult population.

Reflecting on Sri Lankan women's political participation Swarna Jayaveera observed. "The fact that the world's first Prime Minister came from Sri Lanka overshadows the minimal participation of women in national political activities. A highly visible elite is seen in just a position with the low status of majority of women and their marginality in the economy and social values relegate women to an inferior status in family and in society" (Radhika Coomaraswamy, 1990).

Feminist Movement in Sri Lanka

The UN Development Decade however, conscientised about their suffering between the two roles; they benefit from and are also victims of country's development policy. They gave birth to new women's movement in Sri Lanka aiming for a radical change of society towards principal participation of women and self-reliance of poor women.

Despite sluggishness in women's movement in Sri Lanka till 1975, Women's Development Decade has altered the situation significantly. The credit goes to Sri Lanka for forming Asia's first feminist group *voice of women* in 1978. This group has taken up problems of women workers in villages, on plantations, in export processing zones, migrant women in the Middle East, violence against women, images of women in the media and many other issues faced by Sri Lankan women. Hema Gunatilaka, a lecturer at Kalaniya University and a feminist activist in her keynote address at the Davas Conference concluded, "the struggle of women for change cannot be isolated from the struggle of the poor and the oppressed in any society. Women's struggle should be linked to the common struggle against oppressions in all forms".

The Sri Lankan feminists rarely discuss or debate on the possibility of legalizing abortion. It may be due to the fact that in traditional societies the bond between mother and child is still considered sacred and few would advocate abortion in public, regardless of one's personal view in this regard. The success of family planning in controlling the national birth rate might have focussed public discussion on "prevention measures" rather than "abortion".

To sum up, the circumstances peculiar to Sri Lanka stalled emergence of women's movement on a notable scale till 1975. However, this trend has been reversed with the emergence of first Asian feminist group in Sri Lanka in 1978.

Women's Movement in Africa

To understand the women's movement in Africa, South African case is considered. South Africa provides a unique opportunity to observe in a contemporary setting. A process of rendered construction of what it means to be a worker and citizen and gendered understanding of what working class and political organisation should demand (Siedman, 1993).

Women are not organised along sexual lines in South Africa. Women's movement can be considered as entirely absent from the South African social fabric primarily due to the race factor. While women share with the white man in the exploitation of the blacks, black women who have an intuitive understanding of the exploitation and devaluing of their men rebounds upon them. Women's organisations or women's movement must be viewed in terms of the dichotomy, which inhibits sex or simple class fraternities and reacts against feminist coalitions.

Black women have to seek the permission and approval of father/husbands etc. for doing practically anything other than attending to domestic duties and their wage labour. They generally tend to support the activities undertaken by their men. Women's organisations in South Africa are mostly subordinate wings of male bodies encouraged by men to provide services like tea making, fund raising etc.

Early Organisation of Women and Women's Movement in South Africa

Christianity played a significant role in bringing South African women together. The church has organised African women in urban areas into what are called Manyano. Manyano, the African women's organisation draws women of all tribes, responds to women's needs and looks after the welfare of the poor.

Though non-political and welfare oriented in nature Manyanos have transformed themselves into protest groups against apartheid. They resisted the extension of passes to women in 1913 and 1950. They defended women's rights to brew beer in 1940. They agitated against the expropriation of African-owned properties and forced removal in 1954 as well as statutory inferiorisation of African education in 1955. Manyano remains the most authentic African women's organisation. In fact, the African National Congress Women's League (ANCWL) was not only modelled on the Manyano but also largely supported by it. It is said that the success of 1956 Pretoria pass demonstration was largely due to nation-wide Manyano networks. Manyano largely represents the relatively uneducated unskilled workers mostly in domestic employment. The Young Women's Christian Association (YWCA) largely organised the relatively educated and economically well off African women by incorporating black chapters around 1950's. Its African component dominated black provoked tension and resulted in its split.

African Women's Support for National Liberation

In 1952 women from the National Indian Congress (NIC) and the African National Congress (ANC) joined and established the Durban and District women's league. The league actively participated in 1952 campaign of defiance of unjust laws. It organised protest movements when passes were introduced for African women and around 600 women both African and Indian were arrested.

The league representatives were among the founding members of the federation of South African women at Johannesburg in 1954. The league sent 156 representatives, when 20,000 women took an historic march on Pretoria in 1956, organised by the federation of South African women. In 1960, the league organised protest march of women and children of those detained in Durban during emergency. It also organised weekly vigil outside the prison to focus public attention towards imprisonment without trial. However, the banning of it secretary in 1954 and its chairperson in 1960 and the banning of ANC and key members of NIV weakened and split the demise of the league.

Again in 1972, after a gap of a more than a decade a National Indian Congress (NIC) began organising women on a new and non-racial political basis by founding women's federation, Natal. However, due to opposition for inclusion of white women, since 1975 it functioned as a federation of black women. It held a three-day conference at Durban focussing on black family. It drew around 300 delegates representing 10 women's organisations and groups. The federation organised ministries covering key areas viz., education, franchise, housing, women's disabilities etc. It also took steps to start its branches in rural areas. The federation was actively involved when violence erupted in Saveto in 1976.

Developments Since 1975

A notable development in the South African women's movement was greater entry of young women into the fold of women's organisations in contrast to earlier domination by older married women. The focus of the women's movement since 1975 remained broadly liberatory but there is a consciousness of ideological issues of feminism, class and race. However, women have not pressed for their demands till they attained independence in 1990. The emerging changes in South Africa particularly changes in the roles of women since 1970's had its impact on women's movement and the nature of articulation of their demands.

Although African women are mostly concentrated in unskilled and low paid jobs, they got integrated into the industrial labour force and attained an unusual degree of economic independence. South African's migrant labour system has eroded the peasant economy and conditions of social production have undermined the male-dominant household patterns. Urbanisation in the 1970's increased pressures on African women to find paid work given that subsistence agriculture was impossible. Over 1980 formally registered a third of African women in South Africa registered in work force. Patterns of African women's employment also changed in rural areas during the 1980's due to unhealthy politics of creating new possibilities for industrial employment for African women living outside urban centers. Women's participation in trade unions which was there since 1950's became more vigorous after legislation of unions in 1979. Reflecting on women's participation in union activities in late 1970's onwards Frances Bard, a veteran unionist and leading communist activist observed "we know that there is no freedom for the men without the women (Siedman, 1993).

Thus during the year 1980, as rightly observed by Siedman "in the context of broad public mobilisation, changes in women's labour force participation rates and in household patterns have led black women to question assumptions of domestic subordination. Especially in the labour movement and within community groups, there is clear evidence that many black women believe a post-apartheid state should respond to gender specific concerns, women activists, often organised in semi-autonomous women's groups and supported by the international spread feminist ideas and assistance have increasingly raised what Maxine Molyneux (1986) calls "strategic" gender issues, questioning gender inequality within political organisations, within work places, and even within the domestic arena (Siedman, 1933).

The Christian women's movement formed in 1982 under the auspices of the South African council of churches is overtly anti-apartheid and faintly feminist. On feminist levels it asserts. "we are concerned about eh church's reluctance to allow women to participate fully in the life of the church. We are recognised as fund-raisers and tea-makers, but the gifts and skills we can bring to the policy-making bodies of the church are seldom recognised" (Fatima Meer, 1987).

The feminist movement has yet to make an impact on African women. Seidman observed few South African women easily accept the label "feminist" even now, but problems of gender relations and household issues have increasingly been included in broader debates within the anti-apartheid movements.

Seidman observes: feminist demands within the South African nationalist movement emanate not from a few educated women or the national leadership but from within precisely the popular base from which the NAC draws it support.

To sum up, African women's movement has come a long way from the tea-making and fund raising Manyanos of 1950's to ardent protagonists for women's economic independence and personal autonomy by 1990's.

Women's Movement in Latin America

It is difficult to generalise across countries in a region as diverse as Latin America. Latin America and Caribbean region consisted of 13 countries viz., Argentina, Bolivia, Brazil, Chile, Columbia, Costa Rica, Equador, Guatemala, Jamaica, Mexico, Peru, Uruguay and Venezuela. However, an attempt is being made to present a broad picture for a better understanding of the situation.

Latin American nations are plagued by chronic economic and political crisis. Under both civilian and military rule, traditional conceptions of women's roles on the one hand, western Christian families on the other, were at the core of national security ideology, counter insurgency and regressive social practices. However, there is a wide divide between the state discourse on gender and family far from the reality of women's lives. While official discourses extolled the virtues of traditional womanhood, regressive economic policies forced millions of women into the work force. Further female victims of state repression were brutalised, sexually violated and humiliated and subjected to abuse in stark contrast to the military's exaltation of feminists and motherhood. By the late 1970's in countries ruled by civilian and military men alike, reactionary social and political policies sparked widespread opposition movements, women of all social classes deified their historical exclusion from political activities and joined the opposition in unprecedented numbers. To illustrate, in Peru in 1980's working class women were in the forefront of grassroots survival struggles and they challenged the social and economic policies of the conservative civilian administration of Belaunde Terry. Gautemalan women who suffered more than three decades of brutal repression under military coup which started in 1954, participated in the arduous struggle against repression and injustice in 1980. Similarly, during the 1970's in military ruled Argentine, Chile, Uruguay and Brazil women participated on a large scale in the opposition's struggle for democracy and human rights.

Economic crisis also has driven working class women to diverse collective survival strategies. Under the influence of Catholic Church and the male left, women's groups have shouldered responsibilities like providing basic necessities of life consistent with their traditionally defined roles. They also took lead in the day-to-day resistance strategies of Latin American popular classes. In almost every country in the region women have participated disproportionately in movements to secure better urban services to protest the rising cost of living and to secure health care and education for their children. Torture, disappearance and other reforms of political repression also united women of all social classes to organise human rights movements.

Both the above types of movements are commonly referred to as movements de mujeres (women's movements) or *movimientos femininos* (feminist movements).

Feminism in Latin America

Latin American feminism, is part of a larger, multifaceted, socially and politically heterogeneous women's movement. In most of the Latin American countries, feminists initially gave high priority to working with poor and working class women. They helped women organise community survival struggles.

Paradoxically, feminist merged in Latin American history during the 1970. The origins of the feminist movement in Latin America reflect the characteristic of a large sector of the female middle class, rebellions and doubtful of the traditional patterns that marks their destinies. They are mostly intellectual women, with considerable political experience throughout the 1970's mostly among the "New Left". The Latin American females, inspired by modernism, demanded universal equality as the basis for women's full citizenship. They not only challenged patriarchy and its paradigms of male-domination— the militaristic or counter insurgency state—but also joined forces with other opposition groups in denouncing social, economic and political expression and exploitation.

The second-wave of feminism in Latin America was born of the "New Left", as women's issues were often relegated to secondary position in the male dominated Latin American progressive and revolutionary movements. Feminist consciousness was fuelled by multiple contradictions experienced by women active in guerilla movements or military organisations, student movements. Early radical Latin American feminists retained a commitment to radical change in social relations of production—as well as reproduction while continuing to struggle against sexism within the left. Many early feminist groups functioned clandestinely—as-front groups for left-wing opposition or avoiding the term 'feminist' while forming women's associations. Not to alienate themselves from the potential mass base, early Latin American feminists also shunned political work or even discussing issues such as sexuality, reproduction, and violence against women or power relations in the family. They are also deterred out of fear of losing legitimacy in the eyes of the left male comrades in struggle who label man-hating feminism, as bad feminism which has no place in Latin America.

Even though many Latin American women espouse feminist beliefs, they are reluctant to embrace feminist label for fear of admonition by Catholic Church and left-pioneers I organising many popular women's organisations but deliberately blocking the development if a critical gender consciousness among the participants of the *movimientos de mujeres*.

Latin American feminists see their movement as part of the continent's struggle against imperialism. Feminism has taken a variety of organisational forms and has combated women's oppression in the full range of political, economic and cultural arenas in which patriarchal domination is embedded. Latin American context of economic dependence, exploitation and political repression resulted in intersection of gender-oppression and other local forms of exploitation and domination in feminist political projects.

Over time after establishing a mass base among working women, feminists got out of the left notion of bad feminism. As the ranks of feminism grew, Latin American feminists redefined the prevailing notion of a revolutionary struggle. They are asserting that a radical social transformation must encompass changes not only in class but in patriarchal power relations as well.

Thus, Latin American feminism today is a politically and socially heterogeneous movement composed of women who identify with feminism but who retain an unwavering commitment to socio-economic justice and popular empowerment. Women from all social sectors, with wide ranging personal and political views now call the movement their own. It has also emerged as a distinctive political identity which in turn empowered women to exert their impact on public policies, political and social organisations.

Comparative Perspectives of Women's Movement in USA and Sri Lanka, Africa and Latin America

In terms of origin, women's movement in USA originated in their quest for equality with men while in developing countries like South Africa and Latin America, it originated as a struggle for survival in the depressing economic conditions on the one hand and state repression on the other. Ceylon stood on a different footing with total absence of any women's movement till the organisation of the voices of Sri Lankan people in 1980 by a feminist group.

In all the countries under study, women's movement originated in the urban areas and only later it spread to other parts. There are differences in the social background of the women participants. Latin American women's movement is mostly a middle class movement for equality at the work place and the homefront. In Sri Lanka it is limited to elite women's claim for positions in politics on a limited scale. On the other hand, it is a mass based movement of uneducated and unskilled workers for survival and independence in Africa and Latin America.

Women activists in the United States did not retire from public life after the ratification of the suffrage amendment but continued to pursue interdependent aims of complete citizenship and the creation of a feminist welfare state. In Africa and Latin America women have actively participated in the nationalist struggles along with men, without focussing on gender issues. But once the basic goal of independence was won, they have put forth gender issues and claims for equality on all fronts.

While USA is credited for initiating feminist movement in developing countries like Sri Lanka, Africa and Latin American countries, it also embraced it by 1970 and largely by 1980's through contacts with the Western World, and transformation in the socio-economic and political scenarios of their respective countries.

Though feminism has come into being in all the countries under study each has its native influence. While in the US its focus is on issues like sexuality, family life, work sharing, in Sri Lanka the stress is on empowerment and self-reliance of poor women. In Africa feminism has yet to make an impact on women at large though gender issues have come to the force in forums fro anti-apartheid movement. In Latin America, feminists view their movement as part of a larger struggle against imperialism, though feminism has merged as a distinctive political identity on its own.

6

Indian Social Reformers and Advancement of Women

Raja Rammohan Roy (1774-1833)

Raja Rammohan Roy was the father of Indian Renaissance. Universal brotherhood and sisterhood was the aim of his life. Whether he tried for religious reform or desired educational reform of aspired for women welfare or established Brahmo Samaj, his goal remained the attainment of human dignity and freedom. He pined for a society transcending superstition and ignorance. He was a noble individual who led his life with a sublime ideal taking the aid of a philosophic outlook. He advocated the view that ignorance in the country could not be wiped out unless it be with the assistance of Western scientific knowledge. He desired the spread of English language to know the affairs of the world, history and science. He condemned the deep-seated superstitious beliefs, hardened customs, ignorant religious traditions and caste differences as the bane of the country. He had mentioned in 'Vajrasuchi' that these evil factors contributed to the disunity in the country. He raised his banner of revolt against the elite and the 'noble' and be friendly with the untouchables. He strove for an equalitarian society. He went to England to plead for the reduction of the tax burden on poor peasants. He realised the importance and utility of newspapers and founded the first national newspaper.

When all the higher jobs in administration were reserved for Westerners he made out a case for Indians being given high government positions. He was a person of all-round learning and talent. He was a multilinguist who was conversant with ten languages. Besides his papers on geology, astronomy, geometry and other modern sciences he wrote articles on fine arts. During the eighteenth century the condition of women was regrettable. The women were groaning under outdated traditions, superstitious customs, religious orthodoxy, ignorance born out of want of education. They were leading lives like to those of slaves. Polygamy, bride-price, idol-worship, untouchables, human sacrifices and Sati were some of the social evils. There were many innocent mothers who silently wept and bore the tradegy after sacrificing their first born to the river Ganga (Ganges). When the Britishers evinced interest only in business and never bothered to bring about reform of Indian society through education or welfare programmes. Rammohan Roy established a college for women and encouraged women's education. He was anxiety for effecting inter-cast and widow remarriages. He called upon the people to help the widows. He even made an appeal to that effect in 'Sambandhi Kaumudi'. He advocated widow remarriages through his speeches and writings. He appealed to the Government for protection of women's rights. He pleaded for women's right of inheritance. He detested polygamy and described it on the basis of Hindu sastras, as a blot on married life and a slur on Hindu society. He submitted memoranda protesting against polygamy. He specified in his will that his sons or reversioners should not succeed to his self-acquired property if they are polygamous. He laid stress on human rights realising that equality could be achieved only by giving equal opportunities. He knew full well that social progress was chimerical unless it was accompanied by the happiness of women constituting half of the population. He fought for women's social, economic, political and educational privileges throughout his life. He was the equalitarian who admitted the women, depressed classes and foreigners into the Brahmo Samaj when Sudras and women of Hindu society were debarred from study of Vedas. He was the first Indian to advocate elimination of disparity between men and women except in physical characteristics.

Prevention of sati was the first reform. The women of those days used to sacrifice their lives on the funeral pyres of their husbands succumbing to the pressure of the orthodox, whether they believed in that or not. Under the superstitious belief that wife and husband would happily cohabit in heaven 2355 women performed sati during 1815-1817. Those were the days of polygamy. Even those women who never had the privilege of ever embracing their husbands and women residing far away from their lords jumped into the funeral fires holding a stick with turmeric smeared cloth in their hands; they burnt themselves alive. In one word Roy was the person who sowed the seeds of reform of women's condition. He got a law passed in 1829 prohibiting sati as a result of his strenuous struggle. We have to adopt his spirit of fraternity transcending disparities of nation, religion, caste, varna and class. His message is to be remembered forever. The womankind is ever indebted to that noble individual.

Acquaintance with Western Culture

After the advent of Westerners into the country, especially after the Englishmen settled down the Indian intellectuals became acquainted with Western culture. The slogans of the French Revolution, liberty, equality and fraternity attracted the Indians. The secular outlook of the westerners fascinated the Indian minds. The idea that education should be within the reach of one and all gained momentum. The people became infatuated with modernism. Social reform movements sprouted. Brahmo Samaj, Prarthana Samaj and Arya Samaj were such movements.

Brahmo Samaj

Raja Rammohan Roy heralded the movement. He founded the samaj on the principles of worship of one God, moral conduct and search for truth. In 1822 he set up an English school for the spread of English language. He gave importance to sciences and expressed the need to study them rather than follow the ancient mode of education.

Principles of Brahmo Samaj

- Vedas are no authority
- There is only one God
- Prayer is necessary
- Idol worship, oblations to ancestors and sacrificial rites are taboo
- There is no rebirth
- Discrimination on the basis of caste, creed and varna shall be ceased
- Universal human being is the ideal one

Kesav Chandrasen (1838-1884)

As an acharya and a propagandist Kesav Chandrasen developed Brahmo Samaj. He encouraged inter-caste marriages. He insisted on the removal of the sacred thread by the Acharyas. He worked for the betterment of the position of women. He wanted women to go for higher studies. Brahmo Samaj was split into two afterwards. Sadharan Samaj came into existence but its influence dies down gradually. In Andhra Kandukuri Veeresalingam and Raghupati Venkata Ratnam Naidu were leading Brahmos.

Eswara Chandra Vidyasagar (1829-1891)

A Sanskrit college conferred on Eswara Chandra on the title "Vidyasagar". He strove to enhance the marriageable age. He supported widow remarriage. In December 1856 he performed the first widow remarriage. Hindu Remarriage Act came into force in 1856. In Bengal there was a particular sect of Brahmins known as "Kulins". Everyone tried to have alliances with the people belonging to that sect. The kulin Brahmin used to marry many times for dowry. Eswar Chandra Vidya Sagar condemned this system. He longed for the development of women's education. He wished that everyone should study Bengali and English. There were many stories about Vidyasagar regarding his determination to support and perform widow remarriages. He read many scriptures with a view to find authorities in ancient texts to convince the orthodox. He was able to find a sloka in '*Parasara Smriti*' supporting his stand. In the particular sloka it is said, "a woman can remarry if her husband's whereabouts are not known or if he is dead or if he becomes a sanyasi or a depraved person. Vidyasagar convinced some orthodox scholrars with his argument. He wrote two books advocating widow remarriage and the books were sold in thousands in a very short period. There was a wage of support for Vidyasagar's Movement. Many lyrics were printed on the borders of the women's sarees. After he performing the first widow remarriage in Calcutta he performed many similar marriages. He performed such marriage in the case of his only son Narayan Chandra also. This is an instance to prove that he practiced what he preached. We should remember Vidyasagar as a great social reformer who did great social service. Like Eswara Chandra in Bengal, in Maharashtra Vishnu Sastry performed many widow remarriages. Vidyasagar condemned polygamy as it was one of the factors for the increase in the number of widows. Bethune laid foundations for women's education. In 1849 he started a girls high school on his name. Vidyasagar, Madan Mohan, Tarakalankar and other enlightened people helped him.

Dayananda Saraswati (1824-1883)

Dayananda Saraswati upheld *Varna Ashram Dharma*. He pleaded for abolition of castes. He accepted the authority of Vedas. He worked strenuously for reviving Hinduism. He could stem the tide of Muslim influences. Therefore Arya Samaj established by him gained support in Muslim dominated areas of the country. He laid stress on moral character. He condemned child marriages and polygamy. He wanted that Vedas should be within the reach of all sections of the society. He undertook many projects for development of education.

Arya Samaj

Dayananda Saraswati established Arya Samaj in 1875. The principles of Arya samaj are:

- God is omnipotent and omniscient
- Veda is the source of all knowledge
- Truth should be accepted and untruth must be discarded
- All activities must conform to Dharma
- The spread of goodness in physical, social and spiritual sectors should be the goal
- An outlook of love and passion for justice must pervade life of people
- Ignorance should be replaced by knowledge
- Life spent in a self-less way for social welfare should be the aim
- Individual freedom shall prevail
- people can reach God's way through knowledge

Arya Samaj did not believe in *Adwaita*. It did not accept the theory of incarnations. It gave a way to ancestor worship through *sraddha* (ceremonies). It prohibited inequality of sexes. It postulated a *Varna* system on the basis of qualities and actions. It provided for a programme of *Suddhi* (purification) for conversion from other religions. Men and women were given the option to enter any *Ashram* (any stage of life). It helped women's upliftment through reform of Hindu religion.

Mahatma Phule (1827-1890)

Mahatma Phule belonged to Maharashtra. He criticised the hierarchical system of Hindu Society. He questioned the injustice of Brahmin superiority. He denounced the caste system. The non-Brahmin Movement took inspiration from his ideas. He is one of the foremost persons who encouraged women's education. In 1851 he established a high school for women. His wife rendered adequate support to her husband in all efforts at performing widow remarriages and spreading women's education. They were pushed out of the house by his father for undertaking the said activities. Even then he was striving for education of women till the end of his life.

Mahadev Govind Ranade (1842-1901)

Mahadev Govind Ranade gave grater importance to social reform than political reform. He was a judge of the Bombay High Court. He campaigned for elimination of child marriages and performance of widow remarriages. He made propaganda for equal rights to women and their freedom. He criticised the caste system devastatingly. He firmly believed that British rule produced beneficial results. He was influenced by the 'Bhatia Movement'. Even then tolerance of other's views and religion was his forte.

Maharshi Karve (1858-1962)

Maharshi Karve was born in Maharshtra. He took teaching as a profession. Upliftment of women was his chief preoccupation. He lost his first wife and then married a child widow in 1898 educated in Sarada Sadan founded by Pandita Ramabai. He started a shelter for Hindu widows in 1869. Some widows were kept in his own home and educated. He toiled for education of unmarried girls. The *Ashram* which he set up was first named 'shelter for orphan girls'. In 1951 he founded a women's university at Bombay. The medium of instruction was the mother tongue. That education which was deemed necessary to mould women as wives and mothers was imparted to women. The study of English language was compulsory there. Gandhi, inspite of his disagreement with several aspects supported it. Karve toured extensively for the spread of his ideas and for funds. Now the University started by him is known as SNDT women's University. He utilised his full time and energy after retirement for the development of women's education. Many universities conferred him Honorary Doctorates. The Indian Government honoured it by awarding the title 'Bharat Ratna' to him. He died in 1962 at the ripe age of 104 years. The womankind should always be indebted to him.

Pandit Ramabai (1858-1922)

Pandit Ramabai was born in a rural orthodox learned Brahmin family of Maharastra. The place of her birth adjoined the western ghats. Her father was associated with the family of Peshwas. He had an interest in women's education.

Ramabai's first teacher was her mother. She was a child prodigy. By the age of twelve she could recite twenty thousand Sanskrit slokas from her memory. She lost her parents in 1876. Then began her travails. She had to accompany her brother from place to place for a pretty long period of six years. She travelled in the country far and wide. About her impressions she wrote, "we had good opportunity of seeing the sufferings of Hindu women ... This made us think much of how it was possible to improve the conditions of women. We were able to do nothing directly to help them but in towns and cities we often addressed large audience of people and urged upon them the need for the education of women and children".

Ramabai met a Bengali pleader of non-brahmin caste and married him. This was an inter-caste and inter-provincial marriage. This was not to the liking of her near and dear. About two years thereafter her husband died. She remained a widow.

She chose Poona as her permanent place of residence. There she acquainted with the social reformers. Her passion for amelioration of conditions of women was whetted there. She founded *Arya Mahila Samaj* to serve the cause of women. Erelong branches of the samaj sprung up throughout the Maratha region.

In 1882 she gave evidence before commission appointed by the Government of India. She proposed appointment of men-teachers and women-inspectors to further women's education. She further impressed on the commission that the faculty of medicine should be thrown open to women as proper medical treatment could reach Indian women only through women doctors. These statements of Ramabai attracted the attention of Queen Victoria. It came to pass later that Lady Duffein took interest on the subject of imparting medical education to women.

Ramabai realised soon that her lack of knowledge of English was becoming an impediment to her public work. She began to master the language of English. She was helped by Miss Henford the then Superintendent of Girl's School at Pune. This friendship with Ms. Henford, enabled her to visit England to study the educational system there. It may be mentioned that she became a Christian there. She visited United states of America and got many a sympathetic soul to get interested in the plight of Hindu women. She could establish 'Ramabai Association' at Boston with chapters all over the country. The members of the Association agreed to contribute to the up keep of a High Caste Widows Home for ten years. In America she studied the public school system and received training in the kindergarten system of educating children. She could learn about the modes of agriculture, weaving and printing etc.

She returned to India and established 'Sharda Sadan' at Bombay in 1889 with an objective to provide shelter to the 'destitute high caste widows'. Many high caste women and persecuted young widows joined the sadan for education. This was a bold enterprise of Ramabai. Many women benefited by the Sadan.

Pandit Ramabai was careful from the very start of the Sadan. She was apprehensive that her embracing Christianity and running the institution might cause misunderstandings in the minds of sympathisers and supporters. She made it distinctly clear that the school would not actively preach Christianity nor try to make converts.

The Sadan received generous financial support from Christian missionary societies from abroad. Hindu revivalists like Tilak entertained misgivings about the 'Sadan' from the very beginning. A report in a Christian newspaper expressing satisfaction at the fact that two inmates have shown their love of Christianity created consternation among Hindu Orthodox circles. Tilak wrote a protest article in his magazine. The Hindu public was agitated. Even Dr. Bhandarkar and Mr. Justice Ranade had to dissociate themselves with the Sadan.

Ramabai had to shift the centre of activities from Bombay. She started a 'Mukti Sadan' (home of Salvation) at Khadgaon. A 'Rescue Home' was established later. In 1890 there occurred a famine in Gujarat. Pandit Ramabai helped the sufferers. In 1896 she had resources to support 50 girls but she was constrained to admit 300 persons in the Sadan. Later the number of inmates of Mukti Sadan increased to 1900 even though her finances permitted feeding only 600 women.

A school was organised with five classes. Four hundred children were enrolled in the kindergarten section. She brought into existence a training school for teachers and an industrial school with provision for oil pressing unit, dairy, laundry, bakery, centers for sewing, weaving and embroidery. Avenues for those who could labour hard were also there.

In spite of much criticism, sometimes misguided, Pandit Ramabai preserved in her endeavours to bring succour to destitute women and miserable Hindu widows and provide the women with education and vocational training. Her work for the women of Bombay Presidency was remarkable and stupendous. She had illustrated in her life that perseverance will pay dividends. Hers is an exemplary life dedicated to service and women's cause.

Ramabai Ranade (1862-1924)

Ramabai Ranade was born in the year 1862 in the district of Satara of the then Bombay presidency. At the age of eleven years she was married to Mahadev Govinda Ranade who later became a judge of the Bombay High Court and attained reputation as a social reformer.

She had the opportunity to meet Pandit Ramabai. Naturally she was influenced by that great personality. She became an active member of Arya Mahila Samaj. The meetings of the Samaj were held at her house.

No doubt she might have also been inspired by the ideas of her consort. In 1884 she started taking part in social activities. She started a 'Women's Club' at Bombay. She was elected as its President. In the same year she gave her first speech wherein she pleaded for establishment of a Girl's High School at Poona as it was called then. This shocked the orthodox women of the city.

Since 1902 Ramabai conducted the activities of the Women's club at Pune. She opened adult education classes for women and got taught them three 'R's. Vocational Training was given to women such as in sewing. With the efforts of 'servants of India Society', Seva Sadan was founded at Bombay. Ramabai got a branch of Seva Sadan opened at Pune. The Pune Seva Sadan did tremendous work among the poorer class women. It trained women in first-aid, nursing and midwifery. The Sadan sent two young women for training in nursing to Sasoon hospital. She established a hostel for trainees. She toured entire Maharshtra and established branches of Seva Sadan. She got a Seva Sadan opened at Madras. In 1912 Seva Sadan organised Arts and Crafts exhibition at Pune where articles prepared by women were kept on view. In 1918 it became an independent institution. By 1924 when she died there were one thousand women receiving training in several courses run by the Sadan.

Ramabai led the agitation for compulsory primary education for girls. She supported the women's suffrage movement. Lawrence who was a member of the Executive Council and also a votary of the women's suffrage movement said, "there is no council which would not be honoured, graced and helped by the presence of such a woman as one who is known to us all, Ramabai Ranade". As Majumdar Roy Chander and Dutta put it in their an advanced History of India the women's movement which started under the inspiration of Ramabai Ranade has succeeded with a swiftness and to a larger degree that would have seemed fantastic even a few years earlier.

Annie Besant (1847-1993)

Annie Besant reformer, political activist, orator and the president of Theosophical Society, was born on 1st October 1847 in Britain. At the age of twenty seven she joined the National Secular Society of England founded by Charles Bradlaugh. She took part in 'Free Thought' and 'Radical' movements of Britain.

She came to India and strove incessantly for right of expression for women, equal rights, elimination of disparities in wages, provision of midday meal for school children, reform of conditions of labour, formation of trade unions and legislative reforms. She opposed animal sacrifice. She launched a campaign for admission of women into Masonic Movement. Her efforts were crowned with success. She started the 'Home Rule Movement' and pleaded for self-rule of Indians. She castigated social evils like child-marriages, compulsory widowhood and hardened caste system. She argued that each individual should be enabled to preserve his or her physical, mental and spiritual individuality. In the view of God, she exclaimed, there is no scope for discrimination between men and women. She supported the associations and societies working for women's well-being. She created an 'order of sons and daughters of India' in order to create spirit of service and sacrifice among the future generations. She stands like a beacon light in the cause of people, especially women.

Sarojini Naidu (1879-1949)

A poet, orator, reformer and a politician, Sarojini Naidu was a woman of all around talent. Freedom, Hindu–Muslim unity, adherence to Gandhism and service to Gandhiji happened to be her ideals. She played a prominent part in freedom struggle. She enlightened foreigners about the justness of Gandhiji's actions. She could recognise talent and encourage it. She tried to be a friend of Jinnah for the sake of Hindu–Muslim unity. She moulded Jawaharlal Nehru imperceptibly for the future of the country's independence. She followed Gandhiji steadfastly in all his travails and successes. She was gifted with the spirit of equality in all facets of life. Narrow-mindedness and selfishness were foreign to her nature. She had a passion for reform. She married a non-brahmin caste that too of Telugu region. Her political history was a reflection of the struggle for Indian independence. She followed the dictum that fear in the fight for Indian independence is an inexcusable blemish and despair an unbearable sin. She propagated the view that unity was to be found in diversity and apparent in unity. She declared on behalf of Indian people that there could be no spirit of difference between Hindus, Muslims, Christians, Parsees, Westerners, Easterns, Asians and Europeans. She never had any attachment for property and wealth. She was happy in her sacrifice. In 1931 she was the president of a Civil Rights Organisation. Her vision extended to the entire world. Service to humanity was her aim.

Margaret Elizabeth Cousins (1878-1954)

Margaret Cousins born in 1878 in Ireland developed interest in social service from her childhood. With her joining a school founded by Annie Besant as a teacher in 1926 her life became identified with India. Her thoughts centered on the handicapped and the helpless people. She founded a regional institution to improve the conditions of women. Later it was converted into 'women's Indian Association'. With the co-operation of Dr. Muthulakshmi Reddy she established the 'All India Women's Conference'. She worked hard towards the amelioration of the condition of handicapped and depressed sections of the people during her stay in Nilgiri in 1934. She founded a 'Mother's Home for Service' at Kotagiri. She fought strenuously for obtaining drinking water to sweepers and scavengers. She was the first woman to be appointed as Bench Magistrate among the Indian women. She indicated that the accused must be treated humanly during the trail. She was detained as a political prisoner in Vellore Central Jail during 1931-32. Even in jail she devoted her attention to the fellow prisoners. She played an important role in women's Movement as one of the founders of All India Women's Conference.

Kamala Devi Chattopadhyaya (1903-1989)

She was born at Magalore in 1903 in a rich family. She has a passion for fine arts. She was also interested in social reform and politics. She disregarded tradition and disdained participation in religious rites. She longed for modernism. She was a victim of system of child marriage. She became a child widow. When the famous poet Harindranath Chattopadhyaya offered his hand to her, kamala Devi's mother agreed to marry them provided her studies were not interrupted.

At the young age of 16 years she plunged herself into the national movement. She became the president of All India Youth Conference. She led a memorable demonstration at that time. She was arrested many times by the government. Altogether she spent five years in jail. She was a leader of the Congress Socialist Party.

Her acquaintance with Margaret Cousins and blessings of Annie Besant changed the entire course of her life. She took to multifold activities to wit organisations of women's associations, service to women and cooperative movement. Women's movement was intertwined with her life. She led the 'All India Women's Conference' with distinction. She supported the Sarada Bill, popularly called after Sarada who moved the private bill for raising the age of women for marriage. She carried on a virulent campaign in its support. She could impress upon the members of the control legislature the need to facilitate the passage of the bill. She moved the resolution on women's rights at the International Women's conference held at Berlin. She secured a pride of place for dance in the educational curriculum of women. She helped for the establishment of Home Science college at Delhi. She was mainly responsible for emergence of polytechnic colleges for women. Her work on behalf of family planning and folk literature was no less great.

She nourished the various fine arts including music and drama. She served for the cause as president of Sangeeta Nataka Academy (Academy of Muslim and Drama) and chairperson of Children's Book Trust. For a long time she devoted her time and energy to handicrafts movement. Her contribution to the rehabilitation of handicrafts in India was immense and memorable. It will be evergreen in the memory of the Indian people.

Whatever activity she undertook she carried on the tasks with initiative, sincerity and self-confidence. She was always looking at any project of her work with an altruistic outlook. Selfishness was foreign to her nature. Name and fame, awards and titles were never sought after by her. She was given the Ramsasy Award and UNESCO Award by Indian Institutions were galore. The awards given by Marathi Natya Parishad (Maharastra Academy of Drama) and Central Sahitya Academy belonged to this category. She was honoured by the Indian Nation and the world.

She was a writer of distinction and merit. She was an orator of eminence. She died at the age of 86 years leaving behind examples of sincerity, sacrifice, steadfastness, sensitivity and service.

Vijaya Lakshmi Pandit (1900-1990)

Vijaya Lakshmi Pandit could obtain education through private study. From 1932 she participated in politics. Doyen of the Nehru family and sister of Pandit Jawaharlal Nehru she could make her mark. In 1935 she was elected as the chairperson of Allahabad Municipal Board and the Education Committee. She became a member of U.P. Legislative Assembly. She was for some time the Minister for Health in the U.P. state cabinet. She acted as the president of All India women's Conference. After the attainment of independence of India she was selected as Vice-President of 'Women's International League'. She was chosen as the leader of the delegation to the 'Pacific Relations Conference' organised by the 'Indian council of World Affairs'. During 1947 and 1948 she led India's representatives at the 'United Nations'. In 1953 she was chosen as the President of the 'General Assembly' of the 'United Nations'. She was the first woman to hold that office. She attained the highest honour that a woman could come across. She was well-known for her service to the cause of women.

Dhanwanti Rama Rao (1893)

She was born in 1893 at Hubli. She worked for sometime as a lecturer in Queen Mary's College at Madras. She joined the 'Women's Indian Association' and took active part in the struggle for women's voting rights. She participated in women's development movement.

During 1927-28 she was the secretary of 'Child Marriage Abolition League'. She addressed many meetings in England on 'The Women's Movements in India'. She led the Indian delegation to the conference of 'International Alliance of Women'.

In 1938-39 she was looking after the Durban branch of Indian Women's Association. She returned to India in 1941 and became the president of the Bombay branch of 'All India women's conference'. She visited America and Japan and studied the Women's Movement. After the attainment of independence of the country she took steps to establish a branch at Bombay of 'Planned Parenthood Association'. In 1952 she organized the Inter national conference of 'Planned Parenthood Association'. She was the person who convened the 'International Conference on Child Welfare' at Bombay. She was elected as a member of the 'Committee for Family Planning Programme and Research'. She attended the fourth international conference of Planned Parenthood at Stockholm. In 1954 she established many centers in rural areas to work for family planning. She was chosen as the chairperson of Advisory Board of 'Association for Moral and Social Hygiene' set up by the Central Social Welfare Board. In that capacity she could strive for amelioration of helpless and hapless women. She was essentially known for her monumental work in the cause of family planning.

Hansa Mehta (1897)

Hansa Mehta who served as Vice-Chancellor of Baroda University was born in 1897. In 1924 she married Jivaraj Mehata the reputed physician and nationalist.

While she was president of 'Bhagini Samaj' (Sister's society) she established the periodical by name 'Bhagini Samaj' and worked as its editor. She was actively participating in child welfare activities, programmes for education of women-workers and running of working women's hostel.

She served for the cause of women by acting as president of 'Gujarathi Stree Sahakara Mandali' (Gujarathi Women's cooperative Society). She joined the All India Women's Conference and became its president for 1945-46). At that time she submitted a paper on 'The Rights of Women' to the U.N. Sub Commission on behalf of India. From 1947 to 1952 she represented India on the 'United Nations Human Rights Commission'. She helped for the establishment of 'Lady Irwin College of Home Science'. She got 'Home Science Faculty' opened in Baroda University during her tenure of office as Vice-Chancellor. She wrote several books for children in Gujarathi language. She left her profound stamp on history by her variegated activities.

Fatima Ismail (1903)

Born on 4th February 1903 Fatima Ismail passed matriculation examination. It was unfortunate that the system of purdah prevented her from taking part in social work till she attained the age of 34 years. Later she served as a teacher in an 'Industrial Training Centre for Adult Women'. In 1936 she was selected as the secretary of the Shimla branch of All India Women's conference. She devoted her attention to the health of pupils. She was a founder member of 'All India Village Industries Association'.

In 1946 an incident caused the turning point of her life. That year her daughter was stricken with polio. Thus her attention was diverted to lame children. Then onwards rehabilitation of disabled children became her ideal and life-work. She established a society to carry on that task. She constructed a hospital to render help through physiotherapy to the handicapped children. By 1952 it became a fifty bed hospital. It was the first of its kind in India.

In 1951 she attended the Second International Polio Mylytis Congress as Indian representative. She attended the fifth congress of the 'International Welfare Association for the Handicapped' at Stockholm. She went to England to appraise herself about the measures to help the polio victims at various hospitals and 'Rehabilitation Centres'.

She could carve out for herself an honourable place in the ranks of those who served for the cause of polio victims.

Maniben Patel (1904)

Maniben Patel was the daughter of Sardar Vallabhai Patel 'The Steel Man' of India and the reputed Home Minster in the first Union Government of 1947 who contributed a lot to the unity of the country. She gave up her school education in order to devote herself to social and political activities. She participated effectively in the constructive programme of the congress along with Kasturba Gandhi and Anasuya Ben. She was a member of Rastriya Stree Mandali from 1951 to 1953. She was the trustee of 'Navajeevan Trust' and 'Mahadev Desai Memorial Trust'. She was connected with Kasturba Memorial Trust. She was the chairperson of the 'Vidyalaya Committee' (Education Committee) of the above Trust. She was an active member of 'Gujarat Vidyapeeth' and 'Birla Mahavidyalaya'. She was a member of the Central Social welfare Board from its very inception. She exhibited great interest in the schemes and the measures for women's welfare taken up by the Board. She was an unostentatious worker of congress persuasion for cause of women.

Rameswari Nehru (1886-1949)

Rameswari Nehru's passion for the progress and welfare of women was proverbial. It was she who was responsible for starting Mahila Samithi (Women's Association) at Allahabad to awaken the women. She published a magazine 'Stree Darpan' (women's mirror) continuously for sixteen years to bring the women's issues to the notice of the public.

Ms. Rameswari was appointed by the Government as member of Consent Committee. She assisted in drafting a report of the views of the people in respect of marriage. She acted as president of 'Indian Women's Association' and vice-president of 'Committee of women's Affairs'. She toured European Countries, Russia and Australia and enlightened the people about social problems in general and women's problems in particular.

She was a founder member of Delhi Women's League. In 1940 she was selected as the president of All India Women's Conference. In the same year she formed 'Children's Aid Society' at Lahore and continued to be the president of the same till 1947. She took up the office of Honorary Director of the Women's Wing of 'Ministry of Relief and Rehabilitation' and discharged her responsibilities very conscientiously. She worked as All India President of Association of Moral and Social Hygiene.

In recognition of her services in the cause of women she was awarded of Padma Bhushan by the Central Government.

Abala Bose (1864)

Abala Bose was born in 1864 in a highly cultured family of Bengal. She was the sister of Chittranjan Doss a patriot, acclaimed as 'Desh Bandu' (friend of the country). She married the great scientist Jagdish Chandra Bose.

She helped Brahmo Girls School to grow in stature and popularity. She instigated her noble husband to offer one lakh of rupees for education of adult women.

She founded 'Nari Sikash Society' (Society for training of women) in 1919. she derived inspiration from Iswara Chandra Vidya sagar to work for the welfare of widows. She founded 'Vidya Bhavan' and through that institution trained widowed women in handicrafts so as to enable them to rely upon themselves. She set up a school for training teachers in their mother tongue. She extended her activity to cover not only widows but also married or unmarried women. She helped for the establishment of 'Mahila Silpa Bhavan' (a school for training women in handicrafts).

Her name will be remembered with love and respect by those who have regard for women's welfare. A special mention was made of her welfare work in the Report of the Government of Bengal (1927 to 1935).

Mahatma Gandhi (1876-1948)

"As long as men and women do not have equal rights and women are treated as unequal at birth it is tantamount to hair of the country being emasculated. Suppressing women is nothing but smoothering the principle of Ahimsa. "I won't compromise on the question of women". These are the words of the Mahatma who awakened women with his encouragement. He was a great religious humanist. He argued that there would not be any progress in the country unless equal representation is given to weaker sections, schedule castes and women in social, economic and political affairs. He was the man of his age who fought for Indian women groaning under superstitions, social ills and the tyranny of husbands. He recognized that injustice was being meted out to women and hence included upliftment of women as an important part of his constructive programme. Thus he had contributed to the resurgence of women.

Mahatma Gandhiji felt pained and anguished that man-made laws, customs and conventions and Dharma Sastras were oppressing women. He opined that only when social rules and laws were made after mutual consultation and co-operation could do justice to women. Men had been dominating women without realising that women should be looked upon as friends and companions. He was of the view that women had not been using their rightful place in society due to ignorance and lack of education. If they were educated they could have played their role in the social, economic and political spheres of the society with intelligence and efficiency. He counselled his followers to take up the programme of educating the women as the first and foremost task. Women were enamoured of their jewels and ornaments due to ignorance. They did not realise that they were really shackles. He opined that adornment will ensue on account of service with a good heart. He felt that ornaments would not enhance the beauty of women. He denounced the system of '*Kanyadan*' (offering the bride to the bridegroom by the father). Nobody had the right give away the girl endowed with individuality. He abhorred the usage of taking dowry by men. He advised the youth to do away with that custom. He was the generous and noble person to call upon the youth of the country to marry the evacuee women who were subjected to sexual molestation. He preferred separation between spouses to coercive cohabitation without love and affection. He thought that break up of moral code was more unwelcome than that of marital tie. He argued that marriage of a girl during her childhood was no marriage at all. He encouraged right thinking persons to marry child-widows. He was against compulsory widowhood. Compulsory widowhood was unholy according to him. He questioned the practice of '*Purdah*' (wearing of veil by women and their seclusion from men). Men had no right to question the women about chastity if a similar rights were denied to women. He observed that woman was reduced to do forced labour at home though she was described as a 'queen of the household'. In his considered opinion both men and women were born with the same intellectual and spiritual capacities. Demeaning of the status of either person in the marital bond would bring about incompleteness of the personality of the other. Thus he strove for equality of status for men and women.

Gandhiji endeavoured till the end of his life for the liberation of women from tradition, superstition, ignorance and lack of education. He expressed the view that men and women were complementary to one another. He could see difference in sex only in that light. He attacked the prevalent notion of men being masters of women.

His outlook regarding women's upliftment was that real reform consisted in eliminating the defects in women's character. Thousands of women plunged themselves into the 'Salt Satygraha' (campaign against salt laws of the British Government) and courted imprisonment inspired by his exhortations. They picketed liquor shops and braved 'lathi' (similar to baton used by police) blows of the police. They donated their ornaments to the funds raised by him. Gandhiji would be remembered for awakening women and inculcating ideas of reform in the minds of women.

M.N. Roy (1888 to 1954)

M.N.Roy who was a terrorist at first and later became a nationalist to change ere long into a Marxist ultimately breathed his last as a humanist. As a prominent follower of Marx who proclaimed the equality of men and women in all spheres of life he endeavoured for the resurgence of women. He condemned the several unjust restrictions imposed on Hindu women in the name of Indian culture. He stated that "people cannot be free while denying liberty and equality and justice to women". He was a seminal thinker. He laid bare his views on women in the book 'Ideal of Indian womanhood'. He pleaded for the people following birth control methods. He had torn to shreds the false views and attitudes towards women. He contributed to the philosophical revolution when he said in that book women could be easily persuaded to believe in the ideals set before them. In course of time their subordination to men, their expropriation, social disenfranchisement, domestic slavery and concubinage assumed the appearance of voluntary self-abnegation inspired by some mystic ideal of womanhood. The glittering gilt of their chains made the slaves happy in their servitude.

Roy ridiculed the view that woman had been given a high position in Hindu society. She was said to enjoy equality with her husband in the spiritual sphere. This was nothing but golden covering of her slavery. Puranas, stories, poems and praises had been covering the reality. As per the tenets of Manu she was bound to exist under the protection of a male. This idea was ingrained in the minds of women. Even women of the present age are not free from this false doctrine. It could be fairly stated that the women's life was a tragedy. It was denoted as a virtue when she silently succeed to the situation. The greater her acceptance of other's domination and the greater her submission she was acclaimed as a virtuous woman. Roy advocated equality of sexes and exposed the hollowness of the theories of the orthodox.

Roy went on in the same vein. He quoted with approval, "As long as there is the slightest ideas of the master and the dependent of the superior and inferior in the hearts of men or in their customs and their practice and laws the consummation of human bliss and evolution which can be found in perfect harmony and cooperation between man and woman cannot be achieved. (Presidential address of Ms. Brijlal Nehru at the annual meeting of Delhi Women's Conference, November 8, 1936).

Roy concluded the book with the exclamation, that "the modern woman does not want to create social chaos. She is only trying to get out of it. Let her not be handicapped by the loadstone of the fictitious ideal of Indian womanhood tied round her neck.

Roy visualised a future for Indian women comprising equality for her, the right to separation and divorce and the right to choose her life-partner. Economic freedom was a must for her. His message to women was that no revolution could succeed unless it is preceded by revolution in ideas.

Dr. B.R. Ambedkar (1891-1956)

Dr. B.R. Ambedkar, the champion of Women's rights fought for elimination of inequalities. He strove for the rights of women and dalits. He was a champion of human rights. His endeavours to ameliorate the condition of women and Dalits were unparalleled. Many reformers opposed child marriages, polygamy, Devadasi system and prostitution. But the credit of resigning his membership of the Union cabinet as a protest against the failure to grant equal rights to women in respect of Hindu law go to Ambedkar. He sowed the seeds for a society free from the system of 'Varna' (caste system) and women's suppression. His efforts did not go waste. He was a democrat supporting the demands of individual freedom and equality. He laid the foundations in the Constitution for a society assuring the same. It was he who proclaimed publicly that he could not have any regard for Hinduism which sustained hierarchical divisions and the caste system.

Ambedkar who belonged to the Mahr Caste of the Hindu society was denied a shave by the barber when he was young. He was asked by his teacher to sit on the floor while the 'higher' caste pupils sat on mats comfortably. In those days the members of 'lower' castes were refused Sanskrit education. Even when he was an officer in the Government of Baroda state the caste Hindu peons disdained to pass on files into his hands. The dalits were prevented from residing in the village proper. These indignities he suffered boiling with rage. The savage scars on his mind due to these several insults were remarkable. They awakened the rebel in him. He could breathe free air during his stay at Colombia University in United States. He benefited much from a study of the works of great masters Rousseau, Voltaire, Ingersoll and Bernard shaw. He entertained revolutionary thoughts and developed scientific outlook. The ideas of upliftment of Dalits and women's liberation germinated them. The few lines in his letter to a friend illustrate the same. The purport of that letter was in essence thus "there is no inequality of sexes in America. Women can educate themselves. They have a right to take up jobs. Therefore they are treading the path of progress. Only when Indian women can command freedom, equality, equal opportunities in all sectors of society then the nation advances forward". He set up an organisation called 'Organisation for Welfare of the Excommunicated' (Bahishkruta Hitakarini Sabha). To bring the activities of the 'Sabha' to public he began publishing a periodical by name Saraswati Vilas.

The efforts of Ambedkar for the rights of women are beyond description. After completing the work of drafting the Constitution, Ambedkar directed his attention to amend the Hindu Law. Hindu religionists were in a majority in the country. Most of them were orthodox. They believed in the existence of Personal Laws. The Hindu Code Bill was introduced on 5th February, 1951. A woman should succeed to a share of joint family property equal to man was the important principle of that Bill. The progressive men and women supported Ambedkar's stand. Many members of parliament including the President Rajendra Prasad and the Home Minister Sardar Patel challenged the propriety of putting forth the Bill for discussion. A Sanyasin by name Karapatra Swamy threatened to contest against Pandit Jawaharlal Nehru. The demonstration of three thousand women under his leadership protesting against the Bill with placards added more fire-power to the opponents. Nehru retreated. A move was afoot to amend the Hindu Law piecemeal and that too in conformity with the wishes of the orthodox sections. Ambedkar became disgusted. He tried earlier to go over to another Ministry. When he could not succeed on the two aspects he resigned his office in the Union Cabinet.

The statement that womankind is indebted to Ambedkar is no exaggeration. This may appear to be absurd to many. In their view Ambedkar tried to ameliorate the condition of Dalits only. They do not know the immense service done by Ambedkar for in the cause of women. This is deplorable.

Ambedkar burnt 'Manu Smriti' (code of Manu) with the understanding that it had perpetuated injustice to Dalits and Sudras (4th Varna of Hindu hierarchy). In reality Manu Smriti harmed not only Dalits but also enabled men to treat women harshly and cruelly. It did not recognise their existence. It smothered their individuality. It granted the right of husbands to chastise their women. It even went to the extent of prescribing the mode of beating. It has categorically stated that woman should always be a dependant.

According to Ambedkar, Manu's aim was to eliminate what little freedom women enjoyed during the Buddhistic period. Manu degraded women. Ambedkar opined that in Manu's view the woman is just a thing. He expressed the view that Manu did not create any new regulations or laws but only reiterated them and gave the social doctrine of suppression of women a new shape ie., made it a policy of the State. Manu did not content himself with just declaration of principles but prescribed injunctions to women. He restricted the women's freedom and created troubles and disabilities for women.

Manu ordained that obsequies and religious rites to be performed for the dead should not be done to women joining anti traditional religious sects, exercising freedom, taking to intoxicating drinks and aborting foetus. Ambedkar openly and publicly stated that Manu, with an aspiration to oppose Budhism, forged chains to bind and thus suppress women. All these ideas were spelt out by him in his essay Rise and fall of Hindu women. The womankind is abound to remember Ambedkar for all time to come.

Sarat Chandra (1876-1938)

Sarat Chandra portrayed the pitiable situation of women through his novels. He depicted the deplorable condition of widows, girls that had been married to men of 'high' caste Brahmins and deserted women. Women's heartening sufferings were brought out prominently in his novels. They provoke the people to ponder over the issues raised. They would enable the readers necessarily to come to the conclusion that such injustices should not be allowed to be perpetrated. He contributed in a large measure to the spread of the powerful idea that women's position should be bettered. His literature translated into many languages was itself a rich tribute to him. Writers of stories and novels are in galore. There are many who have mastered the art of writing. Yet the number of writers who write with a spirit of conviction are rare. They are meager in number. Sarat Chandra belonged to the latter category. He observed how women had been leading their life as a helpless and disowned being. He felt miserable and sorrowful condition of women.

Sarat was just not a compassionate man. He was a thinker also. He put himself the question regarding the why and where for of women's situation. He realised that the woman was considered valueless. He rejected the theories that justified violence and oppression against women. He condemned the selfishness of 'mankind' towards womankind. Generally woman appears in his writings—novels in the role of wife or sister and that too as a widowed sister. Sarat questioned the men regarding the worth of women in their view. He examined in depth the several arguments advanced by Indian man to counter the criticism of Westerners that Indians were not treating women with respect. He scrutinised the system of 'sati'. He perceived the ways of men in making the widow lose her to immolate herself on the funeral pyre of her husband. He observed the manner in which she was disregarded by the society though she was called a goddess. He brought out the heartlessness of an old man marrying a girl just after he lost his wife and prevailing upon his middle aged widowed daughter to serve his second wife. He analysed the thought-process of men in respect system of 'sati'. He exposed the fraud inherent in the propaganda of men that a 'sati' would find a place in heaven. He questioned the men whether they have knowledge of heaven. He laid bare injustices, atrocities and wicked deeds of men against the women. At one point of time it was considered as a virtue on the part of man to offer the wife's company to the guest. This custom prevailed in many countries in the past. He challenged the right of man to gift away his wife's person and honour to the guest of the day. A man could kill a woman. He could dishonour her. This kind of freedom to man, he opined had been resulting in insult to women. The religious preachers declared woman to be the gateway to hell and a reflection of the demon irrespective of her being a mother or a sister.

Even women believed that the rules and regulations imposed on them by men regarding their conduct were meant for their well-being. They were brain-washed by men. Religious heads had ordained that it was the sacred duty of women to observe the marriage laws. Saint Paul pronounced that women should not put questions in the church. All religions gave women a low profile. She was to be worshipped as a mother. Hence the woman was granted the right of motherhood. They were not particular how she became a mother. Motherhood was treated as a necessity. In fact, men whether they were fathers, brothers or husbands all think and act alike in respect of women. Sarat came to the conclusion that religion had taken advantage of self-interest of men to suppress women. The woman who rejected her husband was pushed into the river. If the husband disowned the wife he could get rid of her by paying compensation. At one stage of society man could sell his wife as if she was an article. Widow marriage was banned. It was said that men acted thus to maintain the purity of the society. They alleged that widows were always pondering over the ways and means to get out of the homes. In fact seventy per cent of such women had been leaving their homes on account of lack of food and ill-treatment by their husbands. Women's misdeeds were unforgivable. The case of men was different. They had almost cent per cent immunity. The ancient societies did not provide women with right to divorce. The ancient man did not entertain the notion of allowing woman to exercise the same option. He did not even ponder over it. It was all due to the selfishness of males.

The animal instinct was still preponderant among men. Subjugating women were prevalent in both savage and civilised societies. When the women's position is low in society both men and women will suffer. Some persons think that women being larger in number than men they suffered demotion in society. The idea was wrong and was proved so by the fact of female infanticide. The relation between man and woman should be natural. Sarat was of the firm opinion that it was possibly only through love and affection.

Women considered him as their benefactor. For generations altogether they had been in deep slumber. Sarat could reveal the inherent knowledge, discretion and self-respect of women. Women realised that they were also human beings with likes and dislikes and strove for their own freedom and independence. That was how it came to pass that they entertained feelings of matchless love, affection and regard for him. It was no wonder that he was given a civic reception in 1933 on his 57th birthday. Sarat Babu, the great writer, offered a historic place to the history–less womenfolk. He received praise and appreciation for writing a thought provoking book on women's existence with a spirit of truth-seeking and sympathy towards women.

Premchand (1880-1936)

Premchand was born in the village of Lamhi near Varanasi in 1880 in the family of Srivatsavas well known writers. In his view every woman deserved to be respected. He was married at the age of 15 years. His wife left him after a serious quarrel. She died later in 1904. His friends and relatives pressurised him to remarry. He agreed to their proposal on the condition that he should be allowed to marry a widow. They assented and he married a widow. This was a revolutionary move. He dealt a very heavy blow to the system of dowry by not taking dowry at the time of his marriage. He had referred to the evil practice of dowry at the time of his marriage. He denounced it outright. He suggested grant of succession rights to daughters in the estates of their fathers. He called upon the youth to marry without taking dowry. He propagated that widowers should marry only widows. He is to be revered for his progressive outlook towards women. He translated his ideas into practice and he was to be remembered for this for ever.

Ellen Roy (1904-1960)

Ellen Roy was symbol of humanism. She was a world citizen. At one time she wrote, "My mother is a German: my father is an American. I was born in France and educated in Germany. I married an Indian. To which country do I belong?" For her universalism was an ideal to be translated into practice. Even prior to marriage she was conversant with culture of several countries and political movements. She was influenced by communist thought. She worked as secretary of European section of International Peasant Movement. She had translated the book "Golden Bough" by Fraser into German. She co-authored In man's own image. She was the secretary of Indian Renaissance institute till her demise. She married M.N. Roy only because she was attracted by his intellect, learning and humanist spirit.

Ellen raised the question "whether men and women are different? Are brains dissimilar? Is enlightenment of both sexes at variance?" She opined that the situation of women was intertwined with the entire social system. She advised women to transform the society. She deprecated the tendency on the part of women to be pre-occupied with their problems only. It would be fruitless if women constituting half of the society would leave the problems of the society to be solved by men. They would have to fight for equality of rights, opportunities, dignity and status and take their rightful place in the gigantic task of changing the world. The problems of women were part and parcel of the problem of the society. She called upon women to take part in politics and take up the work of altering the society. Her message given about forty years ago is still valid and deserves our attention.

Maniben Kara (1905-1979)

Maniben Kara is remembered as a leader of the trade Union Movement, a protagonist of the Women's Movement and a veteran of the Radical Humanist movement. Born in a rich Gujarathi family in 1905, she plunged into politics at the young age of twenty. She was never afraid of prison-life. Even in her youth she suffered imprisonment twice.

The Western Railway Employees Union was the centre of her activity. She worked for the welfare of railway labour for fifty years. She had laboured hard for the betterment of their conditions of work and economic status. She introduced a new element into the Trade Union Movement. She impressed upon the labourers that they should not only work for enhancement of their economic status but should be willing to assist the process of development of the society. To this end she called for workers' education. Thus she enabled the workers to discharge their responsibilities as citizens of the country. She trained many workers as Trade Unionists. Recently the Western Railway Employees Union founded a trust on her name called Maniben Kara Foundation.

She had the unique honour of having training in the trade union filed under the veteran trade unionist N.M.Joshi. That served her in good stead. As president of several trade union organisations she has discharged All India responsibilities and duties. She was successful president of All India Trade Union Congress, Indian Federation of Labour, Hind Mazdoor Sabha and All India Railway Men's Federation. For thirty years she continued to preside over the 'Maritime Union with which she was associated but also to the other sister organisations. She served on the executive committee member of International Confederation of Free Trade Unions. She was chosen as a member of the Committee on the Problems of Women labour. She represented India in many international assemblies. 'National Transport Federation' had commended her service in the trade union field. The services rendered by her and her colleagues in 1944 at the time of horrible explosion in the Bombay docks is still remembered.

Her service was not just confined to the labour. She founded the organisation called 'Seva Mandir' (Service Centre) to work for the people in 1929. By her active part in the All India Women's Movement. She contributed to the growth of women's movement. She was a member of the committee appointed by the Union Government in 1972 to study and report on the conditions of women in the country. The Committee report of 1974 stands out as a milestone in the Women's Movement.

When the then world communist leader M.N. Roy came to India Maniben met him secretly and joined his movement. From that time onwards she played an important role as Roy's colleague in the associations founded by him viz. League of Radical Congressmen, Radical Democratic Party and Radical Humanist Movement. She was essentially a democrat in word and deed. Till she breathed her last minute she remained a 'Royist'. She led a life befitting a humanist. She was all sympathy towards the oppressed and tormented.

Maniben remained a spinster. She had dedicated her life to the three movements of Trade Union, women and Radical Humanism. Having led a fruitful and ideal life she died at the age of 74 years. Her death was mourned by workers, women and democrats.

Leelavati Munshi (1899-1978)

Leelavati's service to women and children as the president of All India Women's Central Food Council. Women's Aid Society and U.P. Council of Child Welfare is remarkable. She served immensely for the cause of women. As a member of the 'Council of States' she strove her best to protect the interests of women. Her activities extended to educational, cultural and political fields.

She undertook many programmes and campaigns. Her association with several organisations either as a president or a vice-president and member was noteworthy. She acted as a magistrate of Juvenile court and president of Bombay Children's Aid Society. The organisations with which she had developed intimate relationship are legion in number. 'Bombay presidency Women's Council', 'National Council of Women in India', 'Backward Classes Board of Social Service', 'Ex-service Women's Rescue Home' and 'U.P. Hospital Welfare Committee' were some such organisations. She was a nationalist to the core. In addition she was a literary figure in her own right. Her saga of service was commendable.

Maharani Tapaswini (1837-1907)

She was the daughter of Belur Zamindar Narayana Rao. She was the niece of the patriot Jhansi Lakshmi Bai. She was imprisoned in Tiruchinapalli jail for participation in the Great Rebellion of 1857. After her release from prison she devoted her energies to study of Sanskrit and Yoga. Later she started a school for Sanskrit education in Bengal. She encouraged women to take education. The centre of her activities was Calcutta. Till her death in 1907 she took an abiding interest in women's education.

Swarna Kumari Devi (1856-1958)

Swarna Kumari Devi gained name and fame as a social reformer of Bengal. She was the sister of celebrated poet Ravindra Naith Tagore. She was married at the young age of eleven years. With her husband's she could do away with the strangle hold of 'purdah' system.

In 1884 she took up the responsibility of running a Bengali journal Bama Badhini. She could be described as the first woman editor. In 1886 she formed a women's association. She has laboured hard to establish friendly relations among Indian women. She contributed in a large measure to develop women's interest in welfare activities. She founded a women's ashram to impart education to poor girls. She has moulded the lives of many poor girls to become employees of distinction. She served society during the years 1885 and 1886 as the president of Bengal Branch of Theosophical Society. She attended the national conference of Indian National Congress of 1900 at Calcutta as a delegate. This was the first occasion where a woman participated in the deliberations of the Congress. Amia Bhushan praised her work in the columns of Calcutta Municipal Gazette as follows "The basic steps she took in the amelioration of condition of women are the sole causative factors of betterment of women steeped in ignorance".

R.S. Subbalakshmi (1886-1969)

Subbalakshmi had rebelled against the miserable condition widows. She was the sister of all widows. One incident agitated her mind to a very great extent. Janaki, a child widow could not stand the ridicule of her associates and took refuge in her mother's arms. Subbalakshmi was taken aback as she was widowed at the age of ten years. Her benign father and paternal aunt being cultured persons took her from Tanjavore to Madras to get education. She became a matriculate in 1905 and completed her graduate study in 1911. She was the first woman to became a graduate. In 1913 she received training as a teacher. She joined the 'Widow's Home' at madras.

With the aid and assistance of foreign women Miss Linch and Miss Pager and with patronage of Governor's wife she established many educational institutions to render help to helpless widows. She has moulded many widows as teachers, doctors and lawyers. She infused the spirit of self-confidence in them. There was no discrimination on the basis of caste, creed or race in her institutions. She was considered at first as a social reformer and later she known as an educationist.

Subbalakshmi called upon widows to get themselves educated and stand on their own legs before they embarked on remarriage. Naturally she had to face much criticism. Ultimately the people recognised her sincerity and praised her. As a member of the Madras Legislative Council from 1952 to 1956 she raised her voice in support of education. She fought for adequate salaries to teachers. In 1920 she was awarded the 'Kaiser-e-Hind' medal. In 1960 the Government conferred the title of 'Padma Sree' on her. Her ideals, service and sacrifice have been inspiring social workers all along.

Dr. S. Muthulakshmi Reddy (1886-1969)

The veteran social worker Dr. Muthulakshmi Reddy was born in 1886 in a middle class family of Pudukkota of the then Madras Presidency. She was the first woman to have obtained the degree of M.B.C.M. From her very childhood she was entertaining the idea of her becoming a social worker. As she was the honorary medical officer for widows' Home and Social Service League she was often visiting those institutions. She was an active member of 'Women's Indian Association'. Later she acted as the secretary and president of Madras branch of Women's Indian Association. In 1930 she presided over the Lahore session of 'All India Women's Conference'. She gave evidence before the Lothian Committee and pleaded for right to vote of women. She could ultimately succeed in that effort.

She was intimately connected with 'Sarada Home', 'Women's Home of Service', 'Society of Indian Ladies' striving for protection of minor girls, and 'Madras Maternity and Child Welfare Board'. She contributed to spread of women's education as a member of 'Harteg Committee of Indian Education'. For about seven years she worked as honorary secretary of 'Madras Children's Aid Society'. She evinced a lot of interest in the institutions run by the society viz. 'Juvenile offenders school'. 'women's Home', 'Girls club'. She edited a journal called 'Stree Dharma'. She wrote profusely on women's problems.

As a member of the Legislative Council of Madras Presidency she could get children's wards opened in Kasturba Hospital and Government Maternity Hospital. She got introduced a regular scheme for compulsory medical check up of students, women and men.

It was she who took the initiative for abolition of 'Devadasi System'. She got the 'Hindu Religious Endowment Act' of 1927 amended. Devadasis (Women who were obliged to dance and sing in praise of God during festivals and processions of the diety) owed a lot to her for their emancipation. Other provinces derived inspiration from her in this regard. With to her inveterate industry 'Suppression of Immoral Traffic Act' passed in 1930. At her initiative the then Government of Madras Province passed orders for appointment of house surgeons and medical officers in 'Guindy Institute' to check up the health of the poor suffering from syphilis. She was very intimately connected with 'Avvai Home' striving then for providing protection, education and training to destitute women and orphan children. She had conducted campaigns to educate the people about cancer. She even established 'Camps' for the same. She worked hard for women's progress as president of Madras Advisory Board of Social Welfare. She carved out a place for herself in the Movement for Women's Welfare.

Marry Clubwala Jadhav (1908)

She developed interest in social service from her youth. She worked in the Red Cross Organisation. She had connections with hundred and fifty associations and institutions. She had taken up the managerial responsibility of 'Madras School of Social Work'. She had endeavoured for the progress of many service organisations. She instituted a crèche, a nursery school and medical centre for 'Dalits'. She extended her help to YMCA. She was a member of 'Madras Social Welfare Advisory Board'. The Union Government recognised her valuable services and conferred with the award of 'Padma Sri'.

Kutti Vellodi (1906)

Born in Malabar in 1906 she played a prominent role in the social welfare activities at Hyderabad. During 1905 to 1952 she was responsible for bringing into existence several welfare institutions as the president of 'Indian Conference of Social Work'. 'Home for Lepers', 'Maternity and Child, Welfare Centres', 'Adult Education Centres', 'Slum Clearance Units', 'Family Planning Clinics', 'Hospital Welfare Committees',

'Cafetaria', and canteens were some such institutions. She had rendered help to several societies to extend their activities. By setting up cottage and small scale industries she contributed to the provision of jobs to unemployed. She acted as a member of several committees. She was for sometime vice-president of Delhi branch of 'Conference of Social Work'. She obtained Rs. 1200/- (Rupees twelve thousand only) by a lottery for the cancer hospital. She officiated as a member of the 'committee of campaign for women's savings' of the Central Advisory Committee. She contributed her mite to the cause of women as president of All India Family Planning Association. Service was her motto throughout her life.

Durgabai Deshmukh (1908-1981)

Smt. Durgabai was well known for her dauntless courage and determination. From a semi-educated girl she evolved into a highly educated and respected social reformer. Later she married Sri Chintamani Deshmukh the then Finance Minister of India. The establishment of Central Social Welfare Board stood to her credit. She founded many institutions to cater to the needs of women in distress and to provide education and training for employment. She published a views-paper for women for nearly two decades. She was an agnostic and cared more for 'Dharma'.

Durgabai was born in the Gummidithala family of East Godavary. She was married at the age of eight. At the age of ten years she donated her gold bangles to Tilak fund then being collected by Mahatma Gandhi. She established a Hindi School called 'Hindi Maha Vidyalay' at the age of 13 years. When she was fourteen years old she joined the Congress Volunteer corps on the occasion of session of Indian National Congress in 1923 at Kakinada. As a volunteer at the gate she refused admittance to Pandit Nehru into the pandal as he had no ticket in his hand.

She was working for betterment of the conditions of life of Devdasis, following the path of prostitution and preaching to them to change their lives. She approached a Congress leader Mr. Bulusu Sambamurty who later became Speaker of the Madras Legislative Assembly to arrange Gandhiji's speech for five minutes at a women's meeting. Mr. Sambamurty jokingly demanded Rs.5000 to enable Gandhiji to address the women. She collected the requisite money and paid it in no time. Gandhiji addressed the women for fifty minutes and she translated his speech.

She jumped into the national struggle and was arrested and imprisoned thrice. Once in Madurai jail she was kept in a cell near the cells of prisoners sentenced to hanging. In all she served three years of imprisonment in jail. In those days treatment of the prisoners was much to be bettered.

She founded the institution 'Andhra Mahila Sabha'. Deshmukh's reputation and untiring zeal, the wives of Zamindars and Ranis gave munificient donations to the Sabha. It grew in stature and magnitude. It not only gave shelter to the helpless and needy but trained them as dayas, midwives, nurses, compositors and crafts-persons. Due to the Mahila Sabha women could gain self confidence and develop the urge to lead beneficial and happy life. The Andhra Mahila Sabha had grown to gigantic proportions. It was running colleges for women, vocational courses, hospitals and adult education campaigns.

Durgabai founded a magazine 'Andhra Mahila', a Telugu monthly,. Many stalwarts of the present day women's movement have had the enviable experience of running the journal for nearly two decades. It acted as the vehicle of the voice of women.

As the Chairperson of the Central Social Welfare Board she devised schemes for education of adult women. With to her initiation two-year condensed courses were started by several voluntary organisations of women to prepare the trainees for matriculation examination with the Board's grants and assistance. Vocational courses for women followed suit. She gave dignity and self-respect to voluntary organizations. She strove her best to get the Hindu Code Bill adopted by the Parliament. She gave her unstinted support to Ambedkar in his efforts.

Honours and awards came to her in plenty. Social Welfare Board honoured her and presented a monetry award of three lakh of rupees. She received Gandhi Medal for spreading Hindi. She got Nehru Literary award. She was the recipient of the title 'Padma Vibhushan'. She never claimed credit herself for them. She attributed them to the efforts of her co-workers. She was simple in her attire and high in her thoughts. She used to talk of her associates as colleagues. When she was awarded 'Padma Vibushan' she humbly remarked that there is a lot to be achieved in the social and educational fields.

K. Lakshmi Raghu Ram (1920)

Born and brought up in Duggirala village of Guntur district of Andhra Pradesh, Lakshmi Raghuram developed an interest in service activities at her young age itself. Her temperament favourable towards women's welfare programmes brought her into direct contact with the illustrious social welfare worker Ms. Durgabai. Her acquaintance with Ms. Margaret Cousins also contributed to strengthening of that attitude. When Durgabai thought of a centre at Madras by name Andhra Mahila Sabha to inculcate Andhra women, with ideas regarding service, literature and fine arts it was given to Lakshmi Raghuram to make the venture a reality. She was a founder member of Andhra Mahila Sabha. Many activities were undertaken by the said organisation to enable the distressed and disinherited women to become self-reliant. Lakshmi Raghuram was assigned the task of running an orphanage and educating women. She wrote many articles on women's problems when she acted as editor of 'Andhra Mahila', a monthly periodical published by the association. She had formulated many schemes for women welfare and implemented them. She toured the length and breadth of India to study the situation of women in distress. She found the condition of widows to be deplorable and submitted memoranda to the State and Central governments comprising her views and recommendations. She impressed upon the Department of Social Welfare the urgent need for ameliorative action to better their condition.

She participated in the conference of 'International Alliance of Women' as India's representative. At that time she was the director of Asiatic region. As the president of 'All India Women's Conference' she evinced a lot of interest in the condition of rural women. She could never forget her association with rural life. She was elected as the first president of 'Delhi Andhra Mahila Sabha'. It was only with her interest that 'International Conference of Women' was held at Delhi in 1973. She has carved out a place for herself in the International Women's issues. For five years she was continuously elected as the president of 'All India Women's Conference'. She strengthened that organisation immensely. She has laid solid foundation for the work of that society. She secured a permanent building for the organisations at Delhi. She had been the managing trustee of 'All India Women's Conference'. Even at the age of 65 years she has been actively participating in the 'Ali India Women's Movement' with vigour and wisdom. At her instance the 'All India Women's Conference' spread far and wide. Now it commands the loyalty of four hundred branches throughout India. It has become the major women's organisation in India. Her knowledge, wisdom, vision and steadfastness were always at the disposal of that association. She has set the goals of that association very high and moulded the same into an instrument of 'Women's Movement'. Her spirit of service, interest in women's movement, devotion to the cause of women and perseverance have become 'infectious'.

Veena Mazumdar (1927)

Veena Mazumdar worked in colleges and universities as a teacher of political science. She was employed by University Grants Commission. She was the member-secretary of the committee appointed in 1972 to enquire and report on the conditions of women. The report popularly called 'Status Committee Report' published in 1974. It highlighted the fact that women could not and did not enjoy the rights and privileges accorded to women in the Constitution of India.

Veena Mazumdar could prevail upon the teaching community to take interest in women's problems. She endeavoured to awaken the educated women to the miserable plight of women. She wrote many books on women's problems. She joined the Indian Council of Social Science Research (ICSSR). She was selected as the secretary thereof. In 1978 she became the director of ICSSR programmes. In that capacity, she served as member on various working groups appointed by the Government of India on employment of women, Village Level Organisations of Rural Women, Adult Education Programmes for Women, National Committee on Role and Participation of Women in Agriculture and Rural Development etc. She also served on the preparatory committee for the 'Non-aligned Nations' Conference on Role of Women in Development (Baghdad, 1979), and was an official delegate to the Conference. Dr.Mazumdar assisted in the preparatory work for the Mid-decade UN Conference on Women (Copenhagen,1980) at the request of the Secretary-General Lucille Mair.

In 1990, along with a group of concerned persons, she established the 'centre for Women Development Studies' of which she has remained as director till March 1991. She helped to organise the first National Conference on Women's Studies at Bombay in 1981 and to found the Indian Association for Women's Studies in 1982 of which she became the first General-Secretary. She was part of the Indian delegation at the UNESCO Expert Group on Women's Studies and Social Science Research Council (1986). She has continued as Member of ICSSR Committee on Women's Studies and the UGC Committee on Women's Studies since their inception.

Since 1984, she has served on many other working groups of Government of India for the VII and VIII Five Year Plans and the Conference on Women and Development (Delhi 1985). She was also a delegate at the Conference; she was a member of the Task Force on Training Strategies, Department of Rural Development, etc. She was a founder-Member of International Federation for Women in Agriculture. She served as a member of the Panel of Honorary Advisers and Planning Commission. Her major interests are Women and Development Studies, educational reform and grassroots organising. She could convince the University Grants Commission (UGC) to establish Centres for Women's Studies in all Universities. She participated in many international conferences for women's development.

Social Reformers of Andhra and Advancement of Women

Kandukuri Veeresalingam Pantulu (1848-1919)

First and foremost among the personalities of the epoch of social reform must be mentioned Kandukuri Veeresalingam Pantulu (1848-1919). He was aptly described as the father of Telugu Women's Movement by late Mrs. Kanuparti Varalakshmamma who was the first recipient of the prestigious golden armlet (Swarna kankanam) awarded by 'kesari' of Madras for her contribution to the women's movement. The great intellectual C. Rajagopalachari said "Andhra Desa and Andhra people could not be what they are, if Veeresalingam had not arrived to vitalise them. He was one of the greatest men of India, of keen insight, great courage and dynamic energy. He fought against untruth and championed the cause of progress with Herculean Vigour".

Kandukuri was the first to translate Sanskrit dramas into Telugu, to write satires in Telugu, to translate Shakespeare's dramas into Telugu, to publish a book on 'Physiology for Women', and to wield his pen for the cause of social reform. Veeresalingam wrote 'Satyavati Charitram' to highlight the value of women's education in building a happy home. In his book *'Brahma Vivaham'*, he ridiculed the custom of marrying young girls to aged men. His crusade for marriage of child widows, campaign for women's education, fight against corruption in public life, powerful plea for moral life, his succour to helpless women and his continuous and continual onslaught on the citadel of superstition and ignorance earned for him a place of reverence and endearment in the hearts of all Telugu people. He presided over Social Reform Conferences and persuaded and prevailed upon his colleagues to make efforts to involve their women folk, mothers, sisters and wives in the work. He founded schools and journals to promote the cause of women. In one word, the essence of his life work was the upliftment of women.

Born in an orthodox family, married at the age of ten to Veeresalingam, a young boy of 13, Rajyalakshmi braved poverty and shared life with her husband. She took to social reform with conviction. Her role is not just attachment to the cause of women's progress was passionage and steadfast. She took active interest in the widow marriage movement. She started a school for women and brought hope and cheer to many a young heart among child widows. When the cooks deserted and the water carriers boycotted at the time of a widow marriage, she personally brought water from the river Godavari cooked items of the feast for the guests and contributed to the success of that function. For her to undertake any task in furtherance of the cause she does not need any request or direction. She is there to jump into the breach whenever it is necessary and husband to donate all his property worth Rs.40,000 (imagine in 1906) to Hitakarini Samajam founded by him. Veeresalingam himself acknowledged his debt of gratitude to her by stating that but for her unfailing assistance, he would not have been able to achieve a lot of what he did in his life. As the author wrote in an article elsewhere Veeresalingam had the fortune of having a spirited, committed and understanding woman as his wife unlike Socrates. The saga of struggles passed through by the Kandukuri couple together with perfect understanding and composure, with equanimity and courage and with steadfastness and sacrifice remains glorious forever in the history of the women's movement of our country.

Raghupati Venkataratnam Naidu (1862-1939)

A follower of Veeresalingam, a Brahmo by conviction is well-known for taking up the cause of orphans, untouchables and social purity. Philanthropist in action, reformer with zeal, he provided for shelter to orphans and free education to depressed class children. He made propaganda against nautch parties by 'Devadasis'. He was rightly called a Brahma Rishi. Above all, as principal of Kakinada College he implanted many healthy ideas among the students and moulded their character to the advantage of the society. Venkata Ratnam Naidu paved the way for the reform of 'Devadasi' community.

The most revolting aspect of the evil practice in South India (Devdasi System) was that some of the girls were dedicated to gods in temples so that they might serve as divine servants or 'Devadasis'. They were intended to be God's own dancers and were supposed to be married to a dagger or swrod or to an idol. This prohibited them to seek any further marriage with any man later. The girls were made to believe that if they tried to seek any other way of life, gods would mete out to them most severe punishments. 'They would spend their time in doing religious service to the gods and the devotees of the temple as the word Dasi itself signifies. But as time passed their accomplishments and their beauty came to be prostituted to promote an immoral trade and to drag the unwary youth into immorality. Thus the word 'Devadasi' which had at first a respectable connotation. A servant of God acquired an ignominous meaning of a prostitute. Under such circumstances it was difficult to improve the moral tone of the society or develop respect for women. It is not surprising that the great social reformer Kandukuri Veeresalingam, carried on a vigours crusade against this evil practice in Andhra. His propaganda was not entirely lost on the members of this caste. The eyes of some of them were opened and they began to realisie the harmful character of the custom. Raghupati Venkataratnam Naidu did his best to abolish the evil.

Gurzada Appa Rao (1862-1915)

Another great name which Telugu women can never forget is that of Gurzada Appa Rao. He is remembered mostly for his patriotic songs, songs urging a meaningful life, advocacy of spoken language as the medium of expression for the elite and the learned for his great drama '*Kanyasulkam*' dealing with the sale of girls in marriage by fathers, and lastly for his sympathy with the miserable lot of women, particularly young girls being given away in marriage to old men. His opera *Puttadi Bomma Purnamma* (Poornamma the golden doll) evokes intense feelings of pathos and sympathy. The girl, who was married to an old man, worshipped the goddess before she was to leave her parental home and then committed suicide. Her entreaties to her brother, sister-in-law and mother will evoke sympathy even from a hard-hearted male chaurist.

Gurzada is a writer with a keen insight of social life. He felt pained at the unfortunate condition of women. His ideas were revolutionary. He said "I can very well imagine how the women are suffering as slaves under the authority of men and under the overlordship of men". Elsewhere he pleaded for divorce. He urged the women to arise and awaken. He called upon them to rebel. He said, that woman is not a weakling (*Abala*). Gurzada's passion for women's emancipation blazed forth like lava. His nature was straightforward and honest. He could never brook injustice anywhere much more so injustice to women.

Chilakamarti Lakshmi Narasimham (1867-1946)

Chilakamarti, as he was popularly called outgrew his orthodoxy and shaped himself as a social reformer. He was the contemporary of the illustrious reformer Kandukuri Veerasalingam. As he was the colleague and follower of Kandukuri he could take part in all the movements launched by his preceptor. Chilakamarti gladly accepted the assignment of a teacher in Kandukuri's institutions.

Chilakamarti never followed superstitious practices. He used to think by himself. He never bathed in Godavari during the '*Puskharam*' (finale of the twelve year period to any river). When he was asked by his sister to get out of a cursed house as she lost her husband, mother, son and daughter in that house he refused to budge. He did not mind his sister sending to a relative's house at Vijayawada. Though he was physically blind he proved that he was not mentally blind. He supported the Andhra leader Tanguturi Prakasam when he was excommunicated on the ground that he visited foreign countries. In 1909 he established 'Ram Mohan School' to teach both Telugu and English.

Chilakamarti's greatness was evident from the fact that Kandukuri chose him as one of the trustees of *Hitakarini Samaj*. He acted as president of the Board of trustees' of 'Hitakarini Samaj'. Once during a campaign of fund-raising he collected a donation from a prostitute. He was vehemently criticised for the act of Kandukuri. He justified himself that people should judge an act by the intention implied in it. He opposed the move of Mr. Napati Subba Rao to get religious education included in the curriculum of schools. His outlook was secular.

He encouraged education of women. He got his niece Ravuri Venkata Subbamma educated. She was the first woman to obtain the diploma '*Ubhaya Bhasha Praveena*'. She served as a lecturer in Mary's college at Visakapatnam.He addressed many a gathering on education of women, widow remarriage and eradication of superstitions. He presided over several meetings pleading for reform. He was a reformer in word and deed.

Unnava Lakshminarayana (1877-1958) and Unnava Lakshmibayamma (1882-1956)

Sri Unnava Lakshminarayana and his wife Unnava Lakshmibayamma are names to be cherished by women of Andhra. Lakshminarayana was styled as the counterpart of Veeresalingam in Guntur District. The couple not being content with promoting widow marriages, contributed in a large measure to the awakening of Telugu women by the establishment of '*Sarada Niketanam*' an institution providing educational facilities to women. It is needless to point out that the couple were also the leaders of Gandhian struggle during the days of 'Satyagraha'.

Many women attain glorious heights under the benign presence of their husbands. Lakshmibayamma belonged to a different kind. She could carve out a definite place for herself in the society with her self-effort. She was generally ahead of her husband in the cause of women and did gain name and fame for the Unnava couple.

She was pained at the situation of child widows and became agitated. She pledged her life for their upliftment. Unnava couple stayed at Rajahmundry for one year and imbibed the best qualities of Kandukuri Veeresalingam and his sincere wife Rajyalakshmi. Later they established a 'Widow Marriage Centre' at their native place Guntur in 1902. Same year they promoted and officiated at the first widow marriage. For nearly forty years they participated in the widow marriages as elders by assuming the role of parents.

Lakshmibayamma established a Shelter for the disowned and disinherited Hindu women. It functioned effectively till it was merged in Sarada Niketan. The Unnava couple and renowned Congress man Konda Venkatappaiah were the founders of that organisation but it was left to Lakshmibayamma to manage its activities. To give shelter to widows and to provide education for girls were its main objectives. She undertook the responsibility for raising funds for the construction of buildings for it. She used to travel in a single bullock cart to collect small donations from households for its upkeep and maintenance.

Those were the days of non-cooperation movement. The people of Palnad of Guntur district vowed not to pay licence fee for grazing their cattle in the forest. Lakshmibayamma jumped into the vacancy in the leadership caused by her husband's absence. When Gandhiji visited Andhra area, awakening and dyanamism among women reached superb heights. The women resolved to take part in the 'Civil disobedience Movement'. Lakshmibayamma led the batch of women intent on preparing contraband salt. She was restrained on her way to the sea coast. She was again arrested and imprisoned. Through the journal *Sri Sarada Niketanam* published by her, she had immensely contributed to the spread of ideas of reform.

Lakshmibayamma's personality was distinct and unique. Her tall stature, large face and wide forehead with big cosmetic mark were impressive and unforgettable. Leadership qualities were manifested in her. The serenity of her face used to astound men and women. She was a terror to anti-social elements. She was simple and unostentatious. Her only adornments were her white khaddar clothes. Selfless service constituted her nature. Orphan girls were her found children. Social service was her life-breath. Her craving to reform society was her only wealth. *Sarada Niketanam* was her very life. She had incomparable attachment to it. Protection of the character of women students was her special responsibility. Therefore she took up residence therein. She died in its service. She was indeed a noble woman who led a remarkable life dedicated to service to the country and society coupled with activities for reform.

Tripuraneni Ramaswami (1887-1943)

Tripuraneni Ramaswami known popularly as '*Kaviraju*' is heralded as harbinger of Andhra Renaissance. He will be remembered for his nihilism and positive social reform in respect of the marriage ceremony.

He died in 1943 at an early age of 56. He had put the '*Puranams*' to derision and ridicule. He has dispensed with the idea of "God-hood". He opposed Brahminism and priest-craft in entirety. He propounded the dignity and worthiness of human being. He castigated the iniquitous caste system. He pleaded for social justice. He propagated the theory of Aryan domination over Dravidians being the bane of Indian society. He endeavoured to reform marriage rituals and customs.

'*Kaviraju*' had left behind sufficient number of followers who could later play great roles in the rationalist and Humanist Movements. From a theist he blossomed into a skeptic and ultimately an atheist. Naturally his ideas underwent a great transformation. It is no wonder that his ideas about women were also subjected to change. In a literary piece he pleaded for a woman being subordinate to her husband. He even talked about husband-worship and sexual chastity as desirable virtues in 1930. By 1935 he began to condemn male-domination and male-vices. While he portrayed the character of Sunita, mother of atheist kid Vena he brought out the truth that no revolution was possible without the participation of women. He condemned the slavery of women and the inordinate power of husband over his wife's body. He was all for the education of women. He pleaded for equality of men and women in marriage.

Gudipati Venkata Chalam (1894-1979)

G.V. Chalam had written extensively on social problems affecting women continuously from 1920 to 1950. His writings covered short stories, novels, essays, letters, musings and critiques. He dealt with life of a woman from all possible angles. He questioned the legitimacy of male superiority and the values of male dominated society. He advocated perfect equality between sexes. He protested against the discrimination against women. He condemned the double morality of the society. He has taken up mostly the problems and issues of middle class women. He said, "the society has classified women not as human beings, not as beasts of burden but as things. They have become the property of men". The economic independence of woman is the only way in which she can escape her lord's domination and authority. It is said that even man is a slave by virtue of his employment, economic status and political position. But then the woman is the slave of man and thus slave of a slave. These ideas were propounded and propagated by Chalam. He protested against male superiority in the sexual sphere. The woman owns her body. It needs exercise. She has a mind. It must find scope for thinking. She has a heart. She is entitled to experience. She has sexual desires and aspirations. She must be free to choose the time, place and the person in relation to her sexual urges. Naturally these thoughts of his annoyed and angered the tradition-bound people and those wedded to orthodoxy. He battered at the fort of male-chauvinism. In a way he was successful. He laid the foundations for radical feminist thought in the Telugu country. He is no doubt a complex personality. His ideas are basically sound though it is possible to pick up flaws here and there. It is curious that both some Naxalites and orthodox sections of the society should take to virtual condemnation and rejection of his ideas. Perhaps extreme leftism is inverted rightism.

Chalam struck a blow for sexual freedom of women even as early as 1940. He was well ahead of his times. He peeped into the future with forethought and vision. He is revered and respected as a pathfinder by the modern feminists.

K.N. Kesari (1875-1953)

Born in a poor family at Ongole Kesari became a self-made man. He wished to be self-reliant and hence earned a lot of money by selling his medicines 'Lodhra and Amrita' which he prepared. He entertained the idea that his wealth should be utilised for improvement of the condition of the poor and oppressed. He gave money profusely to women's associations, women's homes and schools. He aided many girl students. He brought into existence a periodical named *Griha Lakshmi*. Most of the pages of the above journal used to contain women's articles. He used to give awards to outstanding women in music, literature and drawing etc with presentation of Griha Lakshmi Gold bracelet. He set apart a sizeable fund for the same. As this award was given annually several women could be honoured. Even now the awards are being given. Many enlightened women of Andhra received the citations and awards.

Kesari published a good number of books on *Women*. He founded *Kesari Vidyalayam* to teach the Telugu students in their own mother tongue. The memorable work of Kesari as an editor of a periodical, lover of Telugu language, educationist and staunch supporter of women's cause will be remembered by posterity. His services to women's movement were noteworthy.

Duvvuri Subbamma (1880-1964)

Duvvuri Subbamma became famous when she took constructive work in Gandhiji's independence movement. She belonged to the first rank of Telugu women who suffered imprisonment during the national struggle. She gained recognition as a first class fighter for freedom.

Subbamma hailed from the village of Kadiam near Rajahmundry. Even though she became a widow at the age of forty five years she devoted the remaining life to serve the nation.

She was an orator of the first grade. She supported the independence resolution moved by Bulusu Sambamurthy at the East Godavary district Political Conference at Kakinada under the presidentship of the renowned leader Tanguturi Prakasam Pantulu. Her speech then was memorable. She participated in the 'Satyagraha' movement in 1921 and was sentenced to one year imprisonment. The then British Government tried its level best to prevail upon her to apologise. She refused to bow down to their wishes. Even from the very day on which she was released she started a whirlwind campaign for Congress Movement. People used to attend meetings just to hear her. She had worked for national regeneration through her propaganda for nationalism for spread of Indian culture and sale of 'Khadi'. She was honoured by the award *Desha Bhandavi*.

She has maintained a national school for women. She participated in the Satyagraha movements of 1921, 1930 and 1932. She became elated when the country gained independence. She could cut jokes freely with Mahatma Gandhi. For sixteen years she continued as a member of All India Congress Committee. She enthused thousands of people by her recitation of poems from classics. She suffered a wild lathi charge in 1942 Movement. In those days when women were confined to homes it was given to Subbamma to take part in national movements and strive bravely in the sectors of social service and social reform.

Kanuparti Varalakshmamma (1900-1982)

Varalakshmamma was one of the few famous women who built up the women's movement in the Telugu land. She endeavoured to spread education and enlightenment among the women for over half a century. She founded *Stree Hitaishini Mandali* at Bapatla in 1933. She attained fame as a poet and short story writer. Her letters to Sarada was educative and informative. She had discussed the contemporary political, social, religious and ethical issues in them. The great philanthropist and supporter of women Dr. K.N. Kesari established the practice of awarding gold bracelet to women of reputation. Kanuparthi Varalakshmamma was accorded the honour of the first recipient of that award. Even though her education was limited to five classes of the primary school she distinguished herself as a dramatist and ballad-writer. She was chosen as a member of the district board. Till the need of her life she remains as a worker for Congress. She brought into existence a library by the name of *Seetha Sadanam*. She could secure a sizeable site to construct a building for her women's organisation. She was regularly organising meetings of women, celebrations on the eve of festivals like Telugu New Year's Day and Sankranti and political functions like Gandhi Jayanti and August fifteenth. It was taboo for women to come into the public in those days. The few women who dared were abused. Some were subjected to cruel treatment. Many used to go over to the Mandali clandestinely. She was performing her task as a protagonist of women's movement freely and fearlessly.

Yellapragada Sitakumari (1911-1986)

The majority of women in Telangana were illiterate. The proportion of illiterates to the entire population of women was only two per cent in 1931. There was no respect for mother tongue. Seclusion (Ghosha) was prevalent in rich families. Under the then deplorable conditions of life it was given to Sita Kumari not only to arrest the growth of superstition and ignorance but also to strive for awakening among women and rehabilitation of helpless and hapless women. She was a constructive social worker par excellence. She was one of the founders of *Andhra Yuvathi Mandali*. Spirit of adventure, generosity and compassion were her virtues. For about four decades she worked as a brilliant teacher in Key's High School in the city of Secunderabad. Education of women and social welfare measures were her foremost interests. Her longing for organisation of women was intense. She was a very effective public speaker. Self-reliance independence and education for women were the three ideals that motivated her. She visualised a new and dynamic society. She provided shelter to about eighty women in distress.

Sitakumari gave training to women for participation in national struggle. In 1957 she was elected as a member of A.P. Legislative Assembly. She was a writer of the first rank. She was second to none in her love of reform and passion for social service. Though she hailed from an ordinary middle class family she never denied her services to any woman seeking shelter, clothing and food all on her own.

Bharati Devi Ranga (1908-1972)

Born at Bapatla, Bharati Devi was the wife of renowned N.G. Ranga, a veteran of the peasant movement. She spread the message of independence struggle far and wide. She is one of the women leaders who took part in the Satyagraha movement in its early stages. She was educated at Sarada Niketanam of Guntur. She gave full support to her husband throughout her life. She took part in the Salt Satyagraha struggle. She was sentenced to one year of imprisonment in 1932. She worked strenuously for the abolition of untouchability. Her services in running the Peasant Institute at Nidubrole were memorable. In 1935 she became a member of All India Congress Committee. She studied in depth the problems of peasants. She lent a helping hand to the handloom weavers movement and students movements. She was elected as a member of Guntur District Board in 1936 and later from 1958 to 1964 she was a member of the Legislative Council of Andhra Pradesh. She was commended by Mahatma Gandhiji for her strenuous work for the cause of social reform.

Gora (1902-1975) and Saraswathi (1911)

The names of Gora couple are familiar to all those who are acquainted with affairs of the world. Though they undertook many programmes they were essentially known as leaders of atheist movement. In fact their lives are multifaced. From social reform to politics there is no programme which they have not taken up. Gora was born in 1902. In his twentieth year his marriage with Saraswathi aged eleven years was performed. Their married life was led with mutual co-operation till Gora died in 1975. Both were born in orthodox Hindu families and both became atheists urged by their search for truth.

Saraswati took part in all campaigns launched by Gora. He served at Madurai, Coimbatore, Colombo, Kakinada and Machilipatnam in various colleges and resigned his jobs on account of ideological differences. Gora did not falter. Saraswati did not protest against her husband's moves. On the other hand she encouraged him. When Gora embraced poverty and decided to lead his life firmly believing in the support by the people, Saraswati, a mother of nine children did not express any fear and doubt.

Saraswati participated in each programme of her husband not as her husband's blind follower but out of her own convictions. She took to reform on her own. She never played the role of a 'shadow of her husband'.

Gora and his wife were not afraid to take up residence in a 'haunted' house at Colombo. Saraswati blasted the superstition regarding the movements of pregnant women at the time of eclipse. Believing in the unity of humankind they shattered the prevalence of differences arising out of various food habits.

Saraswati stood like a rock by the side of her husband, Gora, when he removed the sacred thread from his person proclaiming that the concepts of God and Karma were false and began running a school for Harijans (Dalits). Gora's paternal aunt Jogamma's funeral procession comprised men and women of all castes. It was left to Saraswati to urge Gora to resign his job in the college at Machilipatnam. Their six year of life at Mudunoor relying on the goodness of the people and undertaking adult education, eradication of illiteracy constitute a special milestone in Andhra social life. During that time Saraswati evinced special interest in enthusing women to implement the programmes of eradication of untouchables, elimination of superstitions and getting the women to read the daily newspaper. She assigned to herself the duty of running the hostel. During the 1942 movement she was arrested along with her husband and eldest son. Her eighteen month son stayed with her in the jail at Royavellore.

Saraswati gave up wearing the traditional form of *Bottu* (mark on forehead) bangles and *'tali'* (sacred chain put on by a married woman round her neck). These are progressive acts to some extent. Marrying their eldest daughter Manorama to Arjuna Rao of Dalit community surpasses the rest of their programmes. Though her own mother and Gora's parents opposed the move they got the marriage performed in 1948.

Both Gora and Saraswati established a periodical *Sangham* (society) to inculcate social outlook and another paper called *Arthika Samata* (Economic equality) to foster the idea of equality. Saraswati supported Gora when he contested elections in 1952 to propagate partyless democracy. During the campaign urging the Governor to visit the slums, the government employed hired women labourers to drag her for two furlongs on the road. She was sentenced to imprisonment during the agitation by cultivators of Inam lands. She extended her support to the Bhoodan Movement. She played her role dutifully in the 'Anti-pomp movement'. She also took part in 'destruction of flower plants agitation'. She supported Gora' candidature in 1967 for the Assembly from Vijayawada constituency.

After Gora's demise. She took up a new role. She symbolises Atheist Movement. She was treated as a "mother" by atheist families. Not being content with encouraging inter-caste marriages she gave the inspiration for the inter-caste marriages of three of her children. In the case of many persons, reform stops at their threshold. She is steadfast in her outlook.

Sangam Laxmibai (1910-1979)

Laxmibai lived a full and purposeful life with her ideal of social service, with compassion towards the hapless and helpless and steadfastness in the patriotic struggles. Born in Telangana, then devoid of facilities for education, she went to Guntur to study in Sarada Niketanam under the patronage of Unnava couple with the inspiration of famous leader of Telangana Madapati Hanumantha Rao. She obtained Vidwan degree there. She became well versed in English due to her study in women's college at Madras. She graduated at the University founded by Karve. She was a colleague of Durgabai in the prison at Royavellore as a participant of the national movement. She was a member of the Hyderabad Legislative Assembly from 1950 to 1954. She was selected as Deputy Minister for Education in 1954 by the then Chief Minister of Hyderabad State Burugula

Rama krishna Rao. Later she became a member of parliament and continued for fourteen years. She was one of the three persons selected by Vinoba Bhave to look after the Bhoodan Movement in Andhra Pradesh. She established an orphanage by name *Indira Seva Sadan* at Hyderabad and contributed her mite to the service of the society.

Tehminabai Dhage (1910-1990)

She was born in a Parsee middle class family on 18 June 1910. She passed matriculation examination at Bombay. She obtained B.A. degree from the Aligarh University through private study. She learnt Urdu from Mr.Venkat Krishnaji Dhage, her teacher. During those days feelings of love sprouted between them. As her father did not approve for an inter-religious marriage they could not marry then. At last when he became a chartered accountant i.e. after fourteen years they could marry. This is the peculiarity of their lives. Both were independent in temperament.

Dhage constituted the Hyderabad children's Society in 1950. Later in 1955 Dhage formed an organisation called *Radha Kishen Home* with his own money to provide shelter for orphan children. Another Trust was brought into existence by the name *RadhaKishen Girls Home*. This Trust looked after the children. Dhage was the honorary secretary of these institutions. Till her death on 27 June 1990 Tehmina Bai shouldered the responsibility of running these organisations. The inmates of the home were considered by her as her children. She showered her love and affection on them.

Several elders and leaders used to visit these organisations. Dr.S. Radhakrishnan, Dr.Rajendra Prasad, Pandit Jawaharlal Nehru, Lal Bahdur Sastry, Morarji Desai, Burgula Ramakrishna Rao, Nawab Mehdi Yar Jung were the prominent among them. They were all praise to the work done by them. In 1966 Andhra Pradesh Cultural Department honoured the couple.

Kotikalapudi Seetamma (1874-1936)

Seetamma became well-known as the best disciple of Kandukuri Veeresalingam, the great social reformer. She had the distinction of presiding over the women's conference held in 1913 at Bapatla on the eve of first Andhra Conference to demand the Andhra Province. She addressed many meetings on the problem of widow remarriage. Her speeches were published under the title *Upanyasamalika* (Garland of speeches). She authored a book on higher education for women. She was a theist social reformer. She was appalled by the deplorable condition of women then obtaining in the society.

Nadimpalli Sundaramma (1885-1948)

Sundaramma settled down in Hyderabad when her husband N.Janakiramaiah was transferred to the city from east Godavary district. She had started her hard work for women's progress even before Andhra movement took shape in the Nizam's dominion. In 1915, she formed the *Andhra Sisters Society*. She used to attend each meeting of social work and library movements to spread the massage of women's resurgence and development by her speeches. She was an honorary teacher for twelve years in 'Andhra girl's High School' from its very inception. She had to leave Hyderabad when her husband retired from service. She died at the age of sixty three at her native place. She is remembered as a dynamic woman who sowed the seeds of women's movement in the Nizam's dominion.

Vemuri Saradamba (1881-1898)

She was born in Alluru Agraharam of Gudivada Taluk in 1881. Even at the age of 11 years she wrote the book *Nagajiti Parinayam*. In her '*Madhavi Satakam*' of hundred verses, she portrayed the unenviable condition of women condemned to illiteracy. In those times women used to keep accounts in respect of milk and clothes entrusted to washer-women by signs. She opined in her book that women could attain brilliance not by ornaments but education. She castigated several superstitions. She pleaded for autonomy to women. It was very unfortunate that such an illustrious woman breathed her last at a young age of seventeen.

Ponaka Kanakamma (1896-1963)

Born in village in Nellore District she could become the first woman member of the All India Congress Committee. She served for the national cause as a vice-president of Andhra Provincial Congress Committee. She utilised all her wealth for her participation in people's struggles. She stood like a rock in support of '*Jamin Rytu*' (peasant of estates) a regional newspaper. The cause of peasants was as dear to her as the movement of women. Together with Dronamraju Lakshmibayamma, she established a Girl's School in 1923 in the name of Kasturi Devi. These two women acted as a pair both in politics and literature.

Yamini Poorna Tilakam

Yamini Poorna Tilakam took part in the national struggle and was a member of the All India Congress Committee. She stayed as Gandhiji's guest and this gave her an opportunity to discuss about various women's problems thoroughly. She advocated abolition of Devadasi System. She was a gifted orator and a great scholar. She used to be overcome by uncontrollable emotion when she pleaded in public for the right to marriage for the members of her community. She started a fortnight journal known as *Hindu Yuvathi*. She established an orphanage called *Hindu Yuvathi Saranalayam* at Madras for sheltering young women who wanted to run away from promiscuity to normal life. To help them to earn independent livelihood, training was given in spinning, weaving, basket – making tailoring etc. The Kalavanthulu Associations were formed at Guntur, Narasapur and other places. The first Andhra Provincial Kalavanthulu Social Reform conference was held at Guntur in 1924. steps were taken to implement the resolutions of the conference. It was found difficult to get suitable bridegrooms and so a 'Marriage Board' was started in 1925 to find suitable husbands for girls who wished to give up prostitution and to lead a decent life. Ultimately the Devadasi System was abolished in 1941.

D.V. Ramanamma (1900-1988)

Ramanamma who strove for women's education and women's progress was also a freedom fighter. She was the sister of the celebrated writer Chalam. She brought into existence a women's organisation *Mahila Seva Mandali.* She performed cosmopolitan and inter-state marriages of her children. She was popularly known as a social reformer. The Municipality of Machilipatnam honoured her. She was known as an actress also. She took very great interest in music and literature. She was responsible for the establishment of a women's library and women's hostel at Machilipatnam. She had encouraged her children to become highly educated. She was an indefatiguable speaker on women's issues.

T.Chandramati Devi (1901-1987)

Chadramati Devi's place of birth being Rajahmundry, Kandukuri's influence on her was immense. She was very generous in helping the women's associations. As the president of Sarada Mahila Sangham she has extended number of branches. Red Cross society awarded a gold medal to her for her service to the movement. She played very active role in the women's movement. Being a child widow she had merged her interests and life in social service.

Premlata Gupta (1915-1988)

Premlata Gupta was another name for family planning in Andhra Pradesh. She was a beautiful woman who left her impress on social and educational movements in the State. She was the wife of Mr.L.N. Gupta who was an educational secretary of Nizam's Government. She knew four languages. She devoted her time, energy and money to the progress of manifold institutions which she brought into existence. She was thrift personified. She never squandered money nor did she tolerate wasteful habits of others.

She was the president of A.P. Branch of Family Planning Association of India for a very long period. She was vice-president of All India family Planning Association. She formulated a scheme of 'Training Social Welfare Workers' and started it at Hyderabad. Even though there were many employees, she used to take personal interest in working of the scheme. She received honours and awards from the department of '*Social Welfare and Mahila Navjeevan Mandali*'. She toured entire Andhra Pradesh to spread the message of family planning. She visited several countries of the world to know how family planning was being pursued by them. She conducted orientation training camps, meetings, conferences and workshops in relation to her work towards family planning.

Ms. Premlata was one of the founder-members of 'International Parenthood Association'. She gave full support to the organization of 'Child welfare and maternity schemes'. Her husband was also well-known for his interest in social and cultural movements. Both husband and wife were founder-members of 'Nav Jeevan Women's College'. Mr. Gupta offered his unstinted co-operation to Ms. Premlata. She is to be essentially remembered for her work on behalf of family planning in Andhra Pradesh.

Komarraju Atchchamamba (1906-1964)

Atchchammamba was the illustrious daughter of an illustrious father who contributed a lot to renaissance in Telugu land by his historical tracts, literary works and endeavours for spreading scientific outlook. She is the holder of a degree in medicine and she set up medical practice at Vijayawada. Her home was for several years a shelter and meeting place for members of the top sections of the Communist Party of Andhra. She had close connection with them when she opposed the Zhadanov line which led to taking up of arms by the Communist Party in 1948.

She sent a signed memorandum with 1,00,000 signatures of women urging the Government to amend Hindu Law on the lines of B.N. Rao committee report. Though her residence was at Vijayawada the sphere of her activity extended to the Andhra region. The women inspired by her took up family planning propaganda. Many women began questioning the validity of male domination and male supremacy and characteristics of feudal society. It was to her credit that one thousand women of peasant class could take part in the procession held on the occasion of All India Kisan Conference at Vijayawada in 1944. She broke away from the All India Women's Conference and formed an independent women's organisation with her communist associates. She became a member of the Parliament and worked strenuously for women's progress.

Syamala Devi (1920)

Deriving inspiration from her father she evinced interest in the welfare of women and service to society. For the last forty years she has been participating in social service activities. She has intimate association with 'Gajannana Sevak Samajam, Mahila Vidya Sangham'. 'SwamiVivekananda Education Centre', 'Andhra Pradesh Red Cross, Bharatiya Vidya Bhavan', and 'All India Women's Conference'. She serves these organization to the best of her ability. She has been the secretary of 'Andhra Yuvathi Mandali' for the schools run by it and got constructed buildings to them. She has been running two working women's hostels.

As the president of A.P. Social Welfare Advisory Board she toured the length and breadth of Andhra Pradesh and endeavoured to set up several centers to provide skills and trades to several women. As a member of the Legislative Council of Andhra Pradesh she could represent the aspirations and goals of women.

Josyabhatla Subbamma (1917-1985)

She hailed from a family of orthodox Brahmins. When she was studying third form in Vysya Seva Sadanam at Rajahmundry, the movements of women's upliftment and reform impressed her. As she was left a widow with two children consequent on her husband's untimely death she had to join Dr. Komarraju's hospital as a nurse. Not only did she acquire a lot of training there she could develop interest in the doctor's political life and her programmes for women's progress. She was attracted by the lives of several Communist leaders that were visiting Dr. Atchchamamba. She conceived the idea of devoting her life to the Communist movement.

In 1941 she joined the Communist Party. She married Josyabhatla Satyanarayana, a Communist trade unionist, by exchange of garlands. She started as a Communist Party worker and blossomed into a vice-president of Andhra Mahila Samakhya. She contested the Municipal elections as Communist candidate and was elected. She endeavoured to obtain facilities for women especially water and maternity centers. She was always in the forefront of women's agitations for right to property, child marriage restraint and prohibition of dowry. She used to encourage and promote inter-religious marriages. She has undergone prison-life and underground life. She participated in cultural performances on the eve of conferences. She was acclaimed for her action in the role of '*Venkamma*' in the drama '*Kanya Sulkam*'. She was a person imbued with revolutionary consciousness. She devoted her entire life to the service of the Communist movement and women's welfare and advancement. In essence she was a social reformer.

Ranganayakamma (1939)

Ranganayakamma is the woman who encouraged reform through her literature. She attained name and fame as Muppalla Ranganayakamma at first and later became well known as Ranganayakamma. Her novel '*Balipeetam*' (alter of Sacrifice) got her considerable popularity. She could look at the sufferings of women in the family from manifold angles. As time passed her understanding of women's problems grew. Her ideas got definite form and shape, till she took up the translation of Marx's Das Capital. She gave lot of prominence to women's problems. She wrote novels and stories and depicted women's problems. She accorded immense importance to criticism and self-criticism. Even when her books were going through further editions she used to express her views in each introductions that it would have been better if it had a different way of narration or different ending. Her specialty lay in criticising others' novels or stories. That mode of work sharpened her outlook and contributed to the clarity of her ideas.

The miserable condition of women, the mental suffering of women at the birth of a female child, discrimination in bringing up boys and girls, the sad state of girl children giving up their educational careers, the difficulties in the way of women marrying their lovers, the need for women to act with self-respect in the matter of marriage, the dynamic conduct of women, the nature of love, the capacity for self-determination on the part of women in the matter of marriage, her understanding of nature of dowry, the relationship between love and marriage, male chauvinism, husband's attitude of indifference towards wife's desires and aspiration's husband's control on wife's conduct, husbands non-cooperation with wife, imposing the burden of work at home, husband's unjust exercise of powers over wife, humiliating her before others, his reticence to recognise her individuality, his rejection of her desire to be appreciated by her husband and her conduct in hiding his oppression all these have provided the subject matter of her stories and novels.

She proclaimed that the relationship between husband and wife or lovers is determined by the unison in ideas. After her separation with her husband she has demonstrated that idea in practice. She has declared through her life-style that there is no impropriety in two mature individuals living together as man and woman without going through the marriage ceremony. This has become an encouraging factor to men and women desiring a revolutionary way. Ranganayakamma seems to have become apprehensive about the understanding of the common people and hence laid down restrictions and limitations. She did not take her ideas to the logical conclusion. Any way it is her peculiarity that she could depict the contradictions and evolution of relationship of husband and wife with clarity and completeness. It is her specialty that she could inform the readers through her book '*Ramayana Visha Vruksham*' (Ramayana the vicious tree) that ideas of Ramayana are not useful for the present society. By the time of writing '*Janaki Vimukti*' (Janaki's liberation) her ideas, outlook and her ideology altered. In that book Janaki's brother spoke emphatically, after knowing about her sufferings in her husband's home, that wherever a woman is dependant she does not have freedom, individuality and self-respect.

Vasireddy Sita Devi (1930)

Praising a woman as a '*Pativrata*' (chaste wife) and ideal woman in proportion to the degree of her subservience to male domination happens to be the characteristic of 'Indian woman's culture'. Our film directors and writers have been augmenting that attitude. In contradiction Sita Devi proclaims that true literature is that which sustains woman's individuality and helps its growth by improvement. The seed of these revolutionary ideas found in her novels *Matti Manishi* (Man of the earth) and *Samata* (equality) grew to dixy heights in her novel *Uri Thardu* (the chord of hangman's noose). In the last above mentioned novel the husband of *Karuna* (a character in the novel) calls upon her to earn money for him by prostitution. She casts away the '*Mangala Sutram*' (the sacred thread tied by the bridegroom round the neck of the bride) in her husband's face saying that if it comes to that she would earn money for herself by prostitution and walks out courageously from her husband's home. What the author meant to convey was her abhorrence of such husbands. Sita Devi rejects the doctrine of 'reflection of reality as it is' and voices the aspiration for such reform which values woman's individuality.

One character in one of her stories is a woman who rejects the offer of scholarship for higher studies and sacrifices her life for the service of the rural people and thereby suffers from slander. A person in another story exposes the illegal and corrupt activities of rich people carried on under the guise of women's associations. She has the talent to provoke people to think on the several ideas thrown up by her from time to time in her novels and short stories. Arundhati a housewife subjected to the pressures of a middle class home aspires for the company of Raja Rao who appeared to be a revolutionary and a self-sacrificing servant of the people. She visualises a life of partnership with Raja Rao for ushering in an equalitarian society.

Malladi Subbamma (1924)

Social reformer and activist of Women's movement Ms. Malladi Subbamma was born on 2 August 1924. As both her parental family and her husband's family were orthodox in nature she was performing her duties for about 20 years as a housewife and following the injections prescribed for women. At last she realised her position and took to education again at the age of thirty four years. She has been working for women's welfare and social reform for the last forty years. She could mould herself as a forceful speaker and prolific writer. She published nearly fifty books and about 40 pamphlets on women's problems and women's issues.

She is a builder of institutions. She formed ten societies for advancement and for the cause of women. She established two trusts *Malladi Subbamma Trust* and *Mahila Abhyudaya Trust*. She indulged in agitational activities prior to 1980 when she formed '*Mahila Abhyudaya Samastha*. This society has been organising seminars, lectures and discussions on women's issues. 'Women's Liberation Training Programme', Subbamma Shelter, 'Dowry Offences Investigation Committee', 'Centre for Protection of Women's Rights' and 'Family Counselling Centre' are constituents of *Mahila Abhyudaya Samstha* (Institute for advancement of women). She established '*Abhyudaya Vivaha Vedika*' (Cosmopolitan Marriage Bureau) in 1983 to encourage, promote and officiate marriages transcending considerations of caste, creed, dowry and religious ceremony.

Her monthly magazine *Stree Swechcha* (Women's freedom) is running for the last four teen years. At present it is a part of the activities of '*Mahila Abhyudaya Trust*'. She brought into existence in 1980 a library called "*Mahila Abhyudaya Grandhalayam*". '*Sramika Mahila Seva*' (Association to render financial assistance to self-employed women) by way of loans without interest was formed in 1990.

Her interest in family counselling led her to create a society called '*Family Counselling Center and Marriage Guidance Bureau*' in 1984. She was the first recipient of '*Durgabai Deshmukh Award*' in 1986. She describes herself as "*humanist feminist*".

Role of NGO's and Women's Organisations in Women's Development

Owing to the momentum provided by the national movement in its various phases and more particularly during the Gandhian era, the organisations fighting towards the liberation of women gathered rapid strength. Indian women themselves became increasingly conscious and educated, so they began to realise the cause of their social and economic sub-ordination. In course of time to eliminate the oppression of women the advanced and enlightened sections of women themselves took the leadership of their struggle. During the second phase of women's movement, women established several specific women's organisations led by women themselves, built up their own organisations on an all India scale with a comprehensive programme of social, economic, cultural and political advance of Indian women. These women's originations worked sincerely for the development of women. Greater emphasis on conscientising poor and illiterate women on their legal rights, educating and helping them to achieve and safeguard their rights and education and economic means to enable the sustaining of these aims should find top place on any agenda of women's development. Some of these women's originations run Ballades, adult education centers, vocational training centers, sewing centers, working women's hostels, homes for aged, homes for women in distress, condensed courses etc. Some of the women's organizations and associations started during the latter part of the 19th century are as follows:

National Level

- All India Women's Conference (AIWC)
- Women's Indian Association (WIA)
- National Council of Women in India (NCWI)
- National Federation of Indian Women (NFIW)
- Indian Association for Women's Studies (IAWS)

State Level

- Andhra Mahila Sabha (AMS)
- Mahila Abhyudaya Samstha (MAS)
- A.P. Mahila Sangam (APMS)
- A.P. Mahila Samakhya (APMS)
- Action for Welfare and Awakening in Rural Environment (AWARE)
- Comprehensive Rural Organisation of Social Services (CROSS)
- ANVESHI

All India Women's Conference (AIWC)

All India Women's Conference was founded in 1927 through the efforts of Margaret cousins and others. This is the largest organisation in India with representation of all states. It has a membership of one lakh members in over 400 units. 25 states have a standing committee of 130 members and an executive committee to manage its affairs. The main activities of the AIWC are organising conferences, social welfare programmes and service activities. The first conference (Which was the outcome of a consensus of 22 conferences held in different parts of India in the latter half of 1926) was held in Pune in early 1927 under the presidentship of the Maharani Maya Raj Scindhia of Barods.

Margaret Cousins were its organising secretary. Though intended as a one time educational conference, the delegates decided to have it as a permanent organisation with local constituents, conferences and annual sessions. While the objective of the organisers was to draft a plan for the promotion of education among women in the first conference itself, social reforms also loomed large. The second conference held in Delhi in the year 1928 was presided by Begum Mother of Bhopal and inaugurated by Her Excellency Lady Irwin, Vicerene of India. The third conference was presided by Her Highness Dowager Rani of Mandi. From the fourth conference (Bombay, 1930) onwards the practice of inviting outsiders as presidents was discontinued and an internal member was appointed as president. The first president was Sarojini Naidu. It was in the 5th Conference (Lahore, 1931) the decision to celebrate International Women's Day on 8th March throughout India was taken.

The sixth conference (Madras, December 1931-January 1932) decided to hold a combined meeting of the 3 major women's associations namely WIA, NCWI and AIWC to prepare a joint memorandum for submission to the Franchise subcommittee of the First Round Table Conference. The fifth meeting of AIWC held in 1981 passed a resolution on several subjects. It expressed its concern about the ragging in educational institutions. It demanded ban on export of essential commodities and freezing of the price level. It demanded setting up of Vigilance Watch dog committees to check hoarding black marketing etc. It voiced its abhorrence at the prevalence of themes on violence, sex and crime dominating the film world. It requested for inclusion of more women in the film censor boards. It decided to appoint a committee to go into the question of promotion of peace and education (formal and informal).

Half-yearly conference was held in May 1982 at Gopeswar (U.P.) The conference was perturbed at the increasing violence on Harijan women. It voiced its support to Chipko Movement. The AIWC expressed its deep concern about abuse of children. It demanded the following steps:

- Children should not be exposed to drugs and traffic;
- Laws regarding child labour should be strictly enforced;
- Proper facilities should be made available by Government or local bodies for good and wholesome recreational centers at various levels.

The international alliance of women to which AIWC is affiliated urged its affiliated organisations to press for better access of women to decision-making posts by taking the following measures:

- Eradicating prejudice against women in all walks of life;
- Disseminating information on rights of women;
- Urging government to abolish laws discriminating against women and afford legal protection to women;
- Motivating women to exercise voting rights and participate in political life;
- Removing discriminatory practices in connection with selections, appointments, promotions, conditions of service, retirement and pension rights;
- Equal employment and equal security during periods of involuntary unemployment and educating women for leadership;
- Increasing the representation of women in government, parliament, legislature, local bodies and public posts;
- Reservation of places for women for some time in jobs;
- Educating men and women.

In respect of Health of Women the following suggestions were made:

- Creation of awareness about health, preventive measures against diseases and ill health;
- Emphasising the relationship between employment and health;

- Increasing knowledge about the same;
- Enhancing and facilitating the roles of women and women's organisations in primary health care.
- Promotion of health.

A seminar was held by the Ministry of Labour, Government of India on all India basis on "Vocational Training of Women" in September 1982. The AIWC participated in the seminar. Though the women's participation according to 1981 census was twenty one (21%) only, still greater and greater number of women have entered the employment market. The consensus of the seminar was that "Anything men can do women can do in some cases even better".

Nine women's organisations got together to place their Charter of demands on women's employment before the Prime Minster of the Women's Day of 1983. They expressed their dissatisfaction with pace of progress in ensuring justice, freedom and dignity to women. They demanded immediate action on the following lines:

- Explicit mention of women as a target group in all plans and programmes;
- Substantial expansion of training opportunities for women through (a) reservations, hostels, stipends, child-care facilities and mobile training programmes;
- Establishment of child-care centers;
- Acceptance of motherhood as a national responsibility and effect on extension of maternity benefits;
- Improving enforcement of existing laws through:
  (a) Institutionalised free legal rights and responsibilities of women;
  (b) Educational and communication programmes to disseminate information on legal rights and responsibilities of women;
  (c) Supportive and rehabilitative services to women in distress;

(d) Rigorous enforcement of labour laws;

(e) Associating women's organisations including women subcommittees for enforcement of Labour Laws and for formulating new policies at all levels;

(f) Change in methods of wage fixation and its payment in agriculture and other unorganised occupations to eliminate the discrimination between tasks performed by men and women and to ensure that the wage reaches to the women and not the male head of a group or household;

(g) Regularisation of women contract labourers, special protection to migratory Labourers.

- Legislative and executive directives to:

  (a) Implement government's promise to provide joint titles to husband and wife in agricultural land and house-sites without prejudice to basic principles of land reforms and rights already conferred on women under Personal Laws;

  (b) Establishment of the principle of matrimonial property i.e, equal rights to husband and wife of total assets acquired during marriage.

- Right to work to be enshrined in the constitution
- Establish National Commission on Women with statutory powers.

The All India Women's Conference, the All India Democratic Women's Association, National Federation of Indian Women, Mahila Dakshata Samithi, YWCA and others signed on the memorandum.

Sarojini Varadappa in her presidential address at AIWC is to identify a new set of objectives, new ideals which could once again give it a sense of direction and act as a source of inspiration.

Dr. Usha Mehta in her inaugural address at the same conference in 1982 diplored that Congress Party which promised to give fifteen percent (15%) of seats to women has failed to act. The figure of representation accorded to women never exceeded seven per cent (7%) according to her. She rightly opined that Women's organisations which have till now been mostly concentrating on social work will have to adopt a more militant posture and prepare their members for satyagraha or resistance in case other methods fail.

The AIWC had 420 branches in 1981 and by 1984 it had 500 branches. The All India Journal *Roshini* was being published by AIWC. AIWC had its credit initiating several institutions which have become autonomous by now. Indian Council for Child Welfare, New Delhi, Cancer Institute, Madras, Family Planning Association of India are among such important organisations.

The activities of AIWC and its branches and affiliated organisations extended to programmes for disabled, schools for mentally retarded, family planning, adult education centers, condensed courses, food preservation, wearing, printing press, textile, printing, industrial handicrafts, working women's hostels, labour women, homes for aged, homes for women in distress, schools, dairy and crèches and others.

Women's Indian Association (WIA)

Women's Indian Association (WIA) was founded in 1917 at Madras by Annie Beasant, Dorothy Jinarjadas and Margaret Cousins. WIA was the first women's association in India to bring together all types of Indian women for mutual assistance. The goals of WIA included equality of rights and opportunities between men and women, compulsory primary education for every girl, abolition of child marriages and other social evils, right to vote for legislative and municipal councils on equal terms with men, adequate representation of women in municipalities, taluks, local boards, legislative councils and assemblies and to form women into groups for the purpose of self-development and education and for the service of others.

WIA was the first association in India to make a demand for women's franchise and to a great extent it succeeded in its mission. It organised a deputation of 14 women in December

1917 to wait on Mr. Montague, then secretary of state for India, with a memorandum for the enfranchisement of women and the removal of sex disqualifications for election to all the deliberative bodies. The Franchise Committee had denied extension of franchise to women but the claim was pressed by WIA and its allies. By 1930, women got the franchise in all the provinces of British India though on a very restricted basis. After the attainment of women's franchise, the association began its agitation for their representation in legislative councils.

Ever since its inception in 1917, WIA registered steady growth in terms of both membership and number of regional branches. In 1923-24, WIA had 51 branches and 2500 members. In 1926-27 there were 80 branches and over 4000 members. These branches spread from Kanyakumari to Kashmir. It published a quarterly journal called *Stridharma* which had editions in several Indian languages besides English.

WIA engaged in programmes of social upliftment of women. The most important of these was education. It not only supported the Child Marriage Restraint Act (1929) but also constituted the Sarada subcommittee for the vigorous enforcement of the act. WIA was also responsible to a great extent for the abolition of Devadasi system and suppression of immoral traffic in women.

Another area of social development was adult education, village upliftment and Harijan welfare. The association gave a number of scholarships to deserving girls including Harijan girls. It started and maintained rescue homes and opened an orphanage in Madras.

WIA also developed an international outlook and maintained active links with international organisations of women. It sent delegates to international conferences and also invited outsiders to its sessions. WIA became the parent of All India Women's Conference (AIWC) which was born in 1927. It became the vehicle for expression of the united voice of the Indian womanhood and is the pioneer in transforming women's associations from a revivalist and welfare agency to an equal rights.

National Council of Women in India (NCWI)

National Council of Women in India was founded in 1925 by Lady Aberdeen of the International Council of Women (ICW), Lady Tata and others who had established the Bombay Presidency Women's Council (BPWC). The NCWI linked with the BPWC, the Calcutta Women's league of service and the provincial Women's Councils formed in Delhi, Bihar and Orissa. The major objectives of the National Council of Women in India are as follows:

- To promote sympathy of thought and unity of purpose among women of India;
- To work for the removal of disabilities of women whether legal, economic or social and for the promotion of the social, civil, moral and educational welfare of women and children;
- To organise, develop and coordinate the work of its existing councils and branches and such other councils;
- To co-ordinate the activities of other national organisations of India;
- To form a link with national council in other countries through the international council women.

The NCWI played a significant role in raising the status of women by working for the removal of various legal and social disabilities from which women suffered for centuries. Like other women's organisations, NCWI also stood for women's suffrage and joined hands with them to mobilise support for adult franchise for both men and women and against reservation of seats on the ground of sex.

A major programme of the council was the spread of education of women. The council also engaged in other welfare programmes especially for working women. These included increase in women's wages and maternity benefits. Among its other activities were promotion of women's wards in jails, slum clearance etc. It has contributed substantially to the passing of the prostitution act in Bombay and conducted intensive propaganda in favour of the Sarada Act.

The NCWI was composed of branches and councils in important provincial and state capitals and cities. These units were engaged in field activities which included running of schools, libraries, literacy and handicrafts, rescue homes, orphanages, clinics, hospitals and hostels for women. It has a journal in English language entitled "NCWI Bulletin".

National Federation of Indian Women (NFIW)

This organisation, which started functioning in 1954 made rapid strides due to the loyalty of devoted bands of women activists it could command. It has been trying to involve women more and more in activities aimed at improving their living conditions and social status to heighten their understanding of reasons why they are discriminated against and inspire confidence among them that it is possible to change the existing socio-economic structure by united efforts of the people, men and women both.

The objectives of the National Federation of Indian Women are as follows:

- To strive for the social, economic, cultural and political liberation of women and for their physical, intellectual, moral, artistic and educational progress;
- To ensure the protection of children, the rights of mothers and a happy motherhood for women.

National Federation of Indian Women is another All India organisation of Women. Communists of CPI inclinations supported it. It is also one of the all India organisations in the co-ordination committee to strive for women's freedom. It has a branch in Andhra Pradesh known as A.P. Mahila Samakhya. It holds conference once in two years. It adopts a three-fold attitude. It agitates, educates and organises women. It has been concentrating its attention on:

- price rise
- atrocities against women
- changes in law

- participation in people's struggles along with other people's organisations
- action for peace in and international solidarity
- constructive work
- agricultural labourers

Indian Association for Women's Studies (IAWS)

The Indian Association for Women's Studies (IAWS) was formed in 1982. This association instituted for bringing women together by following academic studies dealing with government policies and grassroot activities relating to women's issues and problems to exchange information, opinions and views and to formulate basic questions to be raised in connection with Women's Welfare and advancement. It is a membership organisation enjoying the patronage and support of U.N. agencies and the government of centre and states in India. It meets once in two years at an important state capital.

The objectives of IAWS are as follows:

- To provide a forum for interaction against individuals, institutions and organisations engaged in teaching, research or action for women's development;
- To provide and establish information centers at different parts of the country for promotion of women's studies and scientific analysis of action for development and promoting women's equality. To this end to develop a network for collection of information relating to teaching, research and action programmes;
- To develop documentation, bibliography and other services;
- To disseminate needed information to all agencies engaged in teaching, research and action programmes;
- To organise periodical conferences to carry forward the awareness and momentum generated by the first national conference which was organsied by the SNDT

Women's University, Bombay, Kanpur University and Centre for Women's Development Studies, New Delhi in April 1981;

- To organise specific action programme for the Development of Women's Studies and perspectives in different disciplines and for the development of appropriate indicators for measuring women's participation in social and economic development;
- To mobilise necessary services and resources with a view to strengthen and assist women scholars, writers and communicators to develop their talents;
- To assist institutions seeking to develop programmes for teaching, research and action for women's equality and development;
- To take up all such action that may be deemed necessary to bring about a change in social values with a view to eliminate attitudinal, conceptual and class biases that hinder understanding of the role and situation of women and their movement towards equality;
- To take up all such action that may be deemed necessary to bring about a change in social values with a view to eliminate attitudinal, conceptual and class biases that hinder understanding of the role and situation of women and their movement towards equality;
- To collaborate with institutions and agencies working for similar objectives at the national and international level.

Since its inception the association has organised eight national conferences in 1984 at Trivandrum, in 1986 at Chandigarh, in1988 at Waltair, in 1991 at Calcutta in 1993 at Mysore, in 1995 at Jaipur, in 1997 Pune and in 2000 at Hyderabad.

Each of these conferences focussed on a particular theme, adopting a modality of a series of workshops around sub-themes. In addition, each conference also had two or three special plenary sessions. In all these conferences, participants are included representatives from neighbouring countries of South Asia.

In addition, the Association also organised an Asian Regional Conference on "Women and the Household", in collaboration with the Commission on Women of the IUAES and the Research Committee 32 on Women and Society of the International Sociological Association. Participants included scholars and activists from various Asian countries as well as large number of Asian Studies specialists from Europe, United States, Latin America and Africa. The Association also helped to organise a regional conference for Hindi speaking states at Kanpur in 1985, on Women and Public Policy.

Besides the above conferences, the Association has under taken, from time to time, organisation of task forces and small workshops on relatively neglected areas with a view to identifying needed action and research strategies. One such task force was appointed soon after the Trivandrum Conference on the basis of a resolution adopted there. It sought to promote research on the Role of Women in the Indian Freedom Struggle. The task force identified research strategies and approaches, bringing them to the attention of research funding agencies such as the ICHR, ICSSR and select Universities/scholars working on the freedom struggle. As a result, both the institutions have stepped up their support to research in this field and a renewed interest has been noted among doctoral students. In 1987, the Association appointed two task forces to examine the implications of the section titled *Education for Women's Equality* in the National Policy on Education, 1986. The first Task Force took up the issue of access to education for the large majority of women who are currently victims of lack of education or discrimination in access. Small diagnostic studies were undertaken in different parts of the courtry on different aspects of this major problem and a workshop was held in July 1987 to identify needed areas for intervention by educational institutions as well as by voluntary organisations committed to gender equality. The programmes of adult education, training/ reorientation of teachers and the use of mass media being implemnted by the Government of India were subjected to an extensive critique on the basis of the evaluative and diagnostic exercises undertaken by different members of the task force. Recommendations were formulated for the Government as well as for the members themselves and were widely publicised through the press and electronic media.

The second task force examined the role of Science and Technology, particularly of institutions responsible for education in this field in promoting gender equality. Since the previous workshops had identified discrimination in access to science education at the school level, the task force undertook some critical investigation in this issue in six selected states, and in the field of professional education in science based areas (e.g. agriculture, technology) at the University level. The findings of this investigation were presented and discussed at a national workshop on "Women, Science and Technology", hosted by the Indian Institute of Science and sponsored by the Department of Science and Technology, Government of India at Banglalore in November 1988.

In April 1985, the Association initiated with the University Grants Commission (UGC) a national workshop on the Organisation and Perspectives of Women's Studies in the Indian University System. In November 1985, the Ministry of Education convened a national seminar on Education for Women's Equality in which the Association was widely represented. Three months before the adoption by Parliament of National Policy on education, 1986, the United Grants Commission issued Guidelines for Development of Women's Studies in Universities, in the drafting of which Association members played a leading role. Since then the Association has taken considerable pains to mobilise faculty support within institutions to accurate the implementation of women's studies.

As a result of its efforts, Women's Studies Centres/Cells have been established in nearly 50 University departments and

Colleges all over India. Research in Women's Studies has proliferated in higher education. As they do so, the close interaction between research and action, between theory and praxis, and between university and community, is emerging as a distinct feature of Women's Studies movement in India. The Association by initiating steps in this direction and by providing space in the form of Conferences and Workshops has contributed immensely.

Over the last twenty years, the Association through its commitment and the work of its members, has been able to carve out a place for itself both within the Women's movement as and within academic centers concerned with educational reform. Its national conferences have been well attended by men and women belonging to various walks of life. The Association has been recognised by the different departments of the government as well as the non-governmental agencies as the most successful mobilising body that can help to identify educational institutions in different parts of the country who can effectively contribute to development programmes involving women as partners, as well as to identify scholars who can take up research in needed areas. The University Grants Commission, Indian Council of Social Science Research and other agencies have established linkages with the Association by giving it representation on their Standing Committees.

Autonomous Women's Organisations of Andhra Pradesh Dealing with Women's Issues

Andhra Mahila Sabha (AMS)

The Andhra Mahila Sabha is the first women's voluntary organsiation in India. It was started at Madras in 1937 as the little ladies of Brindavan. Late Smt. Durgabai Deshmukh was the founder president of Andhra Mahila Sabha. As the days and years passed, this voluntary organisation has grown up into a mighty organisation and the duplication of the programmes were started at Hyderabad in the year 1958 to take up multifarious welfare activities for women's progress. Andhra Mahila Sabha Educational Society located in Delhi is also a wing of Andhra Mahila Sabha.

Andhra Mahila Sabha provides fifty different categories of service. Prominent among the institutions run by it at Madras are Avakasa imparting vocational training to students, "Mahila vidyalaya" with hostel and "Mallamma Devi Mahila Mandiram" helping hapless women who could not pursue their studies to become educated at Iswari Prasad Dattatreya orthopaedic centre. Durgabai was an inimitable builder of institutions. Under her inspiration and leadership educational institutions from kindergarten to post graduate courses sprung up. Nursing home was converted into a big hospital with specialties. A mini-hospital on wheels was set up in Ranga Reddy district.

The services organised by the Sabha are in the field of Health, Medical Care, nursing and education from pre-primary to the college education. The Sabha has contributed to the eradication of illiteracy through adult education and other literacy programmes including functional literacy and non-formal education for rural women leading to the stages of family welfare. Andhra Mahila Sabha has rendered its useful services in the field of social welfare for about 55 years.

The main aim and objective of the sabha is to train women and harness their services for the building up of our nation. Its assets are the selfless and service oriented workers, who dedicated their services to the welfare of thousands of women and children and handicapped laying in their deprived life. Andhra Mahila Sabha is the only voluntary organsiation which has boldly entered into such an adventurous service particularly life saving and giving programmes with service motto.

One of the important services of Andhra Mahila Sabha is the literacy house. Andhra Mahila Sabha is the only voluntary organisation entrusted with state resource centre (Adult education) for producing study materials for illiterates and neo-literates. This centre provides teaching, learning material for the entire state. It has also undertaken non-formal education for rural women. Multi-purpose health workers training programmes, Urban Welfare Centre, Mobile Food and Nutrition extension unit run from 1966 onwards, pre-school training, teachers training, tourist hostel, free legal aid centre, old age homes are other special feature of Andhra Mahila Sabha.

Durgabai emphasised the importance of four pillars (4Ps) personnel, public relations, public reporting and public accountability for service organisations.

Service Centres of Andhra Mahila Sabha

The following are the major service centers of Andhra Mahila Sabha for the welfare of Women and Children at different stages of life:

Sl. No.	*Name of the Centre*	*Year of establishment*
1.	Sisu Vihar for Kindergarden	1957
2.	Vanitha Bala Vihar	1957
3.	Regional Handicrafts Training Institute	1958
4.	Literacy House	1958
5.	The Orthopaedic Centre	1959-60
6.	Nurses Hostel	1961
7.	X-ray Unit and Pathological Laboratory	1962
8.	Nursing Home with Auxiliary Mid Wife Training	1963
9.	Vocational Training and Rehabilitation for Physically Handicapped	1963
10.	Mobile Food and Nutrition Unit	1966
11.	Children's Hostel	1969
12.	Arts and Science College for Women	1970
13.	College of Education	1971
14.	Special School for Orthopaedically Handicapped	1972
15.	Mini Hospital on Wheels	1978
16.	Chintamini Deshmukh Cardio-vascular Unit	1978
17.	Legal Aid Centre for Women	1983
18.	Sericulture Training Unit	1985

Mahila Abhyudaya Samstha (MAS)

Mahila Abhyudaya Samstha was founded by Ms. Malladi Subbamma and her associates in 1980. It is an umbrella organisation striving for all round progress and welfare of women.

In its educational programmes, the samstha held symposia's, seminars, workshops and lectures on issues affecting women. Seminars were held in collaboration with its constituent "Stree Vimochana" on "Status of Women" (1985) "Women and Peace" (1986), "Dowry" (1987) "Obscenity and Impropriety" (1987), "Female Sexuality and Sexual Freedom" (1989) and "Literature, Women, Reform and Revolution" (1992). Its sister society "Abhyuda VivahaVedika" held one seminar on "Marriage Today and Tomorrow (1993). MAS published "Women's Liberation" a feminist manifesto to written by Malladi Subbamma in 1988.

The agitational programmes are noteworthy. Usually MAS takes the first place in launching agitations in the cause of women. Anti-sati Movement (1987), Anti-Monastery Protest (1987), demonstration against Mathamma being unrobed and paraded in the streets of a village (1991), orchestrating dissenting voice over Supreme Court Chief Justice Ranganath Minsra's advice to women not to compete with men (1990), Anti-arrack agitation (1992–93) are some such campaigns.

"Abhyudaya Vivaha Vedika" (Cosmopolitan Marriage Bureau) a sister organisation of MAS encourages, promotes and officiates at marriages transcending considerations of caste, dowry and religious ceremony. "Mahila Abhyudaya Trust (Trust for Progress of women) was founded by Malladi Subbamma. She has been publishing a monthly journal titled "Women's Freedom" for the last fifteen years.

Andhra Pradesh Mahila Sangam (APMS)

The CPM led women had their own organisation called Andhra Mahila Sangam. This organisation is affiliated to All India Democratic Women's Association. A.P. Mahila Sangam had mass membership mostly from the women of proletariat, agricultural labour and poor peasant classes. It contributed its mite towards alleviation of suffering of victims of cyclones of 1977 and 1978 in coastal Andhra by collection of money, rice and clothes. It took a leading part in arranging benefit film shows in aid of Bengal flood victims.

The Sangam took the initiative in bringing into existence an autonomous organisation called "Association for training women in self-defense. This association conducted a training course in Karate for full one month at Vijayawada in January and February 1979. 68 young Women were trained. Booklets were published on 'Cyclone Havoc, Liberation of Women', 'Ideal men and Women' and 'Children's year'.

The Sangam carried on an agitation against atrocities on women. They launched a campaign for punishment of offenders in the case of Shakila, Mulugu Lakshmi and others. It took up the cause of slum dwellers. It roused the conscience of the people against price rise. It helped women withstand the violence of the landlords and police in several villages in the districts of Warangal, Khammam, Nalgonda and West Godavari. Sangam lent its support to the All India Kisan Sangam when it held its council meeting at Palakollu. Likewise it contributed money to "Central Federation of Indian Trade Unions' (CITU) when its All India Confernce was held at Nellore in 1973. Along with other women's organsiations it forged a committee to render help to the victims of fire accidents at Vijayawada and store its best to collect money, clothes, food articles, utensils etc to be given to the needy. It helped women withstand the violence of the landlords and police in several villages in the districts of Warangal, Khammam, Nalgonda and West Godavari.

Notable activity of the Sangam was its pamphleteering and publication of books. Appeal to join the women's movement, Women on the path of Revolution, Veeresalingam and Women's status in India were such publications.

Action for Welfare and Awakening in Rural Environment (AWARE)

This organisation was founded by Mr. P.K.S. Madhavan in 1975. Its area of activities is the territory of six States of India.

It covers 4000 villages throughout the country. Income-generation projects, vocational training, awakening, literacy, adult education, thrift, self-help projects, sanitation, health, medical care, procurement and disbursement of loans, nutrition, ante-natal and post-natal care for women, leprosy relief, flight against superstition, raising of fruit and kitchen gardens happen to be some of the programme of aware for the ignorant, illiterate backward sections of society. It lays stress in serving the hill people and forest dwellers. Its floating hospital on river Godavary with doctors, nurses and attendants serves the medical needs of about thirty riverside villages. It is the first of its kind in Asia. No activity beneficial to the poor is excluded from its purview. Service to women forms its constituent part.

Comprehensive Rural Organisation of Social Services (CROSS)

This organisation with its headquarters at Hyderabad has served the poor and downtrodden sections of villagers in three districts of Andhra Pradesh and in some areas of Kerala and Orissa. Under the dynamic leadership and guidance of Mr. M.Kurian it awakened the people to their plight and organised them for taking up self-help programmes. Organisation of 'Sanghams' (Associations) in villages and Mahila Sanghams (Women's Associations) separately is the distinction of Cross. Enlightenment and education were imparted through adult literacy and adult education classes, discussions, lectures, training camps, orientation camps etc. The women were called upon to fight for liberty and equality, to learn trades, to get training in non-traditional occupations like house-building, motor driving etc. Cross has infused self-confidence among the disinherited sections viz. backward classes and scheduled classes who merited its attention utmost.

Anveshi

This organisation, a research centre for women's studies, has been sponsored by erstwhile activists of '*Stree Sakti Sanghantana*' (Organisation of women's power) of Hyderabad. Actually registered in 1985, Anveshi consists of a group of women from different institutions and disciplines who share a background of activism in the women's movement. It springs from the need for a structures that can nurture and support the creative potential of feminist research which is rooted in the connection between activism and scholarship.

Anveshi runs a library and documentation centre. It holds seminars, symposia and lectures by eminent persons connected with the feminist movement. It sponsored an erudite book on "Forgotten Chapters of Role of Women in Telangana Struggle of 1948-51".

Its sister concern 'Voluntary Health Group' has brought out a compendious volume on health entitled 'Million Doubts and Answers'.

Another study of women who fought for equality, and justice in the past is underway. Two learned volumes are already published thanks to the dynamism of Ms. Susi Tharu and her associates.

Andhra Pradesh Mahila Samakhya

The second Conference of A.P. Mahila Samakhya was held in 1954 at Angaluru of Krishna district. In 1957 Telugu women played host to the All India Conference of National Federation of Indian women held at Vijayawada.

The movement led by Communists had a set back from 1958 to 1964 so far women were concerned probably due to differences in the united communist party in Andhra Pradesh. As such it led to splits in front organisations too. Therefore the women owing allegiance to CPI were constrained to go in for a separate organisation.

In 1970 the Andhra Pradesh Women's Conference was held at Kothagudem. The organisation was named A.P. Mahila Samakhya. It was attended by 1100 delegates representing 10,000 members from 11 districts. There was a procession of 5,000 women and a public meeting of 10,000 men and women. Movement were conducted along with other peoples organisation for waste lands, house sites and land reforms. In peoples organization for waste lands, house sites and land reforms. In

Anantapur 500 houses were built on government land. Sewing centers were set up. Local problems were tackled. 5,000 signatures were collected protesting against high prices in 1972. Picketings, Dharnas and hunger strikes were conducted at fifty centers against high prices and for opening of ration shops. As per the figures of the Samakhya leaders the membership rose to 38 thousands spread in 18 districts. The fourth conference was held at Vakkalagadda in Krishna District. It was attended by 1,000 delegates from 13 districts. Resolutions urging implementation of land, reforms, elimination of social oppression against women, against price rise, and for more jobs for women were passed.

9

International Women's Conferences and Plan of Actions for the Advancement of Women

The scales of world equality are out of balance. The side marked "Woman" is weighed down with responsibility, While the side marked "Man" rides high with power. Advantage builds on advantage until today they are tiled so steeply that almost all of the world's wealth is on man's side, while most of the world's work is on woman's side.

Throughout the world women are treated as second class citizens of the society. They are treated as subordinates to men at every place. As a result, the advancement of women is constrained at all levels. This kind of status has oppressed them of their advancement at all levels. With a view to removing such constraints, the United Nations (UN) which was formed after the victory of the Allies in Second World War and the emergence of independent states following decolonisation were some of the important events in the political, economic and social liberation of women.

The United Nations Decade for Women (1976-85) is an effort to right the scales and first step is redistributing the wealth and the work. The power and the responsibility more fairly between men and women. This observation in the Report on the status of the World's Women, 1985, is a reflection of the new and growing awareness about the condition of humanity struggles for justice and equality in different parts of the globe. Governments of different nations and the UN have started to develop new understanding of who, we as humans are and how, we as global citizens, by our combined and concerted efforts can change the existing inequal power structures. The declaration of the International Women's year, the UN Decade of Women and World Women Conferences from Mexico to Beijing are the manifestations of the vision for a better world and the determination to achieve it.

The mandate to advance the status of women is given in the Charter of the UN. The preamble to the charter declares that the people of the UN were determined to reaffirm faith in fundamental human rights in the dignity and worth of the human person, in the equal rights of men and women and of nations large and small. The Charter of the UN makes the economic and social council responsible for promoting universal respect for, and observance of human rights and fundamental freedom for all without distinction of race, sex, language or religion. The last quarter of this century is marked by a series of efforts towards raising women's status to enhance their quality of life being about gender equality and gender justice.

The effort on the global level was made by United Nations Commission in 1975, the year which was observed as the International Women's Year and 1976-1985 as the International Decade for Women in developing the world plan of action.

First World Women's Conference: Mexico City, 1975

In 1975, a comprehensive statement was made in the Declaration on the Elimination of all Forms of Discrimination Against Women by the Un General Assembly on 7th November 1976. It stated that "discrimination against women, denying or limiting as it does their equality or rights with men is fundamentally unjust and constitutes an offense against human dignity". Subsequently the convention on the elimination of all forms of Discrimination Against Women was accepted by the First World Conference on women in 1975 at Mexico City and adapted by the UN General Assembly on 16th September 1979. At this conference, the following goals were setup by the World Plan of Action:

- Marked increase in literacy and education;
- Equal access to opportunities;
- Increased employment;
- Elimination of discrimination;
- More women in policy-making positions;
- Increased provision for welfare services;
- Part in Civil, Social and Political rights;
- Recognition of the economic value of women's work;
- Promotion of women's organizations within institutions;
- Development of rural technology and support.

The conference resulted in the World Plan of Action for the implementation of objectives of international Women's Year and the Declaration of Mexico on the equality of women and their contribution to development and peace. The World Plan of Action established key areas for national action that included international co-operation and peace. Political participation, education and training, employment, health and nutrition, the family, population, housing and had sections on mass media research and reviewed.

Right after the 1975 conference, the symbol of the United Nations Decade began to be seen even in remote provinces. It transcended the boundaries of cultures, languages and conveyed a simple but powerful message. The symbol was the dove of peace with the women's sign and an equal sign in the body of the dove. New organisations came up with new strategies were recognized, a new consciousness developed a new confidence emerged and new linkages across regions and nations were established.

The resurgence of the new international women's movement contributed to the powerful impact of the declaration of the International Women's Year and the Mexico Conference. The proposal of the International Women's Year was first organisation. Throughout the International Women's year and the two decades that followed, six thousand women participated in Tribune. The parallel non-governmental meeting organized by an NGO (Non-governmental Organisation) Planning Committee at Mexico focussed on the theme of equality, development and peace.

Second World Women's Conference: Copenhagen, 1980

The United Nations covened a Second World Conference on Women at Copenhagen, Denmark from14 to 29 July 1980 to assess the progress made since the first World Conference and to outline actions to be taken during the second half of the Decade for Women (1976-1985). The World Conference of the United Nations Decade for Women focussed on equality, development and peace added three sub-themes to the agenda i.e education, employment and health. Lucille of Jamaica was the secretary-general of the conference. 1326 delegates from 145 countries participated and the document adopted was Programme of Action. The Programme of Action emphasised the importance of equality which means not only legal equality but also equality of rights, responsibilities and opportunities for the participation of women in development both as beneficiaries and as active agents. It also noted that women's development should not only be viewed as an issue in social development but should be seen as an essential component in every dimension of development and peace is a prerequisite to development. Equality, development and peace are interlinked.

The review of work in the past five years indicated that the situation of women in the backward sectors of many countries had in fact worsened. It proved that any measure for women isolated from major priorities, strategies and sectors of development cannot result in substantial progress towards attaining the goals of the Decade. Again legislative and development action unless accompanied by access to information and positive action to change attitudes cannot be fully effective.

During the years between the conferences at Mexico and Copenhagen, the continuing analysis of women's situation revealed that dependency is a vulnerable state. The parallels between the dependency of nations on other nations and the dependency of women on men became clear. The notion of the necessity of increasing self-reliance among women is a much stronger element in the 1980 programme of Action than in the 1975 world plan. It became as stronger theme at the Nairobi Conference. Self-reliance requires organisation, education and training, employment and legislation to put women on the equal footing with men.

Third World Women's Conference: Nairobi, 1985

In March 1983, a special session of the Commission on the status of women was called to begin preparing for the 1985 world women's conference. This conference is to review and appraise the achievements of the UN Decade for women was convened from 15 to 26 July 1985 at Nairobi with equality, development and peace as the primary themes and education, employment and health as sub-themes. The achievements of the decade were reviewed and forward looking strategies for the advancement of women to the year 2000 were adopted by the conference.

The report of the Secretary General on the review and appraisal of the progress achieved and obstacles encountered at the national level in the realisation of the goals and objectives of the UN Decade for Women revealed that the Decade has clearly played a major role as a catalyst in the achievements of legal reforms and overall dejure equality. Among the newer issues were abuse against women and children informing women of their legal rights, legal aid to women and pornography. The report pointed out that "the principle enshrined in international covenants of human rights will only become reality with the determined political will of all Governments. The vision for change was demonstrated at both the United Nations Conference and the Non-Governmental Organisation forum at Nairobi. The adoption of the Forward Looking Strategies on 27th July participating 157 countries in the United Nations Conference was one expression of the vision. The title of the document

'Forward Looking Strategies' for the Advancement of women to the year 2000-is a message with positive connotations.

Special attention was given to education, need for legal changes and their implementation, the linkage of violence against women with the issue of peace and on the recommendation for another world conference before the year 2000. the forward looking strategies are concerned with the equality before law, education, health, employment, sharing of domestic responsibilities by all members of the family, food, agriculture, industry, trade, science and technology, housing, communication, environment etc. Obstacles to effective integration of women in the process of development are continuing arms race, colonialism, apartheid, racism, policies of domination and exploitation, the growing gap between the levels of economic development of the developed and the developing countries, lack of political will of governments to eliminate obstacles, insufficient awareness, discriminating laws and resistance to change the attitudes.

Fourth World Women's Conference: Beijing, 1995

The fourth world conference on women held in Beijing, the capital of the people's Republic of China from 4-15 September 1995 under the ageis of the United Nations on the eve of the fiftieth anniversary of the founding of the United Nations. The theme of the conference was "Action for Equality, Development and Peace". This conference was an important milestone in the history of women's struggle all over the world for equal rights in all spheres of life for a proper standard of living and for a status of equality.

The commission on the status of women has identified critical areas of concern—inequality in the sharing of power and decision making at all levels, insufficient mechanism at all levels to promote the advancement of women, lack of awareness and commitment to internationally and nationally recognised women's rights, poverty, inequality in women's access to and participation in the definition of the economic structures and policies and the productive process itself, inequality in access to education, health and employment and other means of maximising awareness to rights and the use of their capacities, violence against women, effects of continuing national and international armed or other kind of conflicts on women.

After 1975 a world-wide data on the actual conditions of women was generated. Now debates are being raised on some concepts of crucial importance for women like work or violence. The reports and the world conferences have stimulated research on women's issues at national and international levels.

New areas of knowledge like women's studies, Development studies and peace studies have been challenging the very concepts of knowledge, development, power and security. Articulation of demands for peace, justice and equality and the increasing role of the non-governmental organisations have brought new sensitivity to social issues and movements and new networks like AWRAN (Asian Women's Research and Action Network). There have been important conferences, seminars and events like Conference on Women and Human Rights, An Agenda for Unity. New York (1992). Women's Work Banking, 1992, Global Interdependence, Stresa, Italy (1992).

Apart from the research and plan of action across nations, certain definite steps were taken by the United Nations. Two international organisations were formed. One is the International Institute for Research and Training for the Advancement of Women (INSTRAW). It aims at promoting through research and training activities through participation of women together with men in the economic, social and political advancement of society.

A new focus on women has developed within the United Nations agencies like the International Labour Organisation (ILO), the World Health Organisation (WHO), the Food and Agricultural Organisation (FAO) and the United Nations Educational, Scientific and Cultural Organisation (UNESCO). There are also important bodies like the Unite Nations Development Programme (UNDP), the United Nations Fund for Population Activities (UNFPA) etc.

In spite of the effort to improve the status of women the situation is still far from satisfactory. It was brought out sharply by the Report of the World Conference of the United Nation's Decade for Women at Copenhagen which state that "While women represent 50 per cent of the world population, they perform nearly two-thirds of all working hours receive only one-tenth of the world income and own less than one per cent of world property". According to a recent ILO release on "Women in Authority", the Ideal and the Reality only of the United Nations member states are governed by women and women occupy barely 3.5 per cent of ministerial cabinet posts".

In the United Nations like many large corporate institutions women constitute only 3.6 per cent of decision-making elites. In 1989 there were only 337 women (out of 1,695) in the diplomatic staff of the permanent mission and to the United Nations in New York City, sixty missions had no women. Only 8 of these women held the rank of Ambassador. At the VII conference in 1987, there were only 173 women delegates out of 1,375 (13 per cent) and 63 delegations out of 137 included no women. At Fourth Conference of United Nations Development Decade, 15-16 June, 1989 there were 20 women delegates out of 210 (9.5 per cent) and 65 delegates out of 89 included no women.

As the data on discrimination against women from different countries and the United Nations appears, we are aware of different dimensions of inequality operating at different levels. As pointed out by Heliu Sipala the Secretary General of the International Women's Year Conference, the status of women differ significantly from country to country due to cultural, political, economic and social factors.

The global facts collected by United Nations Committee for 1995 World Conference on Women reveals some highlights:

- Violence against women emerges as truly universal issue crossing cultural, geographical, racial, class, religious and ethnic boundaries. Existing laws in many countries offer very limited protection for women. Domestic violence is often regarded as a "private family matter";

- Job opportunities for women have generally been confined to clerks, sales persons, maids, household workers and to the informal sector. They receive lower wages than men for equal work and drop in and out of labour force because of child bearing and rearing responsibilities;
- An estimated 85 to 114 million girls suffer from forced genital mutilation worldwide. (most live in Africa a few in Asia and in recent years cases have been reported even in Europe, Canada and the US);
- More than 10 million women are engaged in prostitution in the world today and 2 million are children;
- Women and girls in both developed and developing countries still do not have equal access to education and training. In some parts of the world, girls and boys now have the same access to schooling and yet imbalances continue.

The most singular achievement of the Beijing Conference was the acceptance by the world community that discrimination begins at birth. The conference made it clear that there can be no rise in the status of women without ensuring that girls are allowed to be born. And once born, the girls should be allowed to grow up into wholesome personalities, with proper education and self-esteem. For the first time there has been a global official recognition of the rights of the girl child.

It has been suggested that in order to improve the status of women and girls in countries like India, China and many of the SAARC countries have to see to it that the spirit of Beijing is kept from the point of view of the poor status of the girl children. Awareness campaigns have to be mounted against female foeticide and stray instances of female infacticide. This is what Beijing meet underscored. One cannot talk of human rights by depriving the basic rights of half of the world population comprising women. The fact that women are not enjoying the basic human rights is explained by the phenomena female of babies being killed before and after birth, neglect of the girl child, dowry in certain parts of Africa, rape and inhuman treatment to widows. The neglect of women is reflected in the adverse sex ratio in many countries including India. The Beijing Conference took an alarming note of what is called "the feminization of poverty" as a result of the impact of the global macro-economic policies on the lives and livelihood of millions of poor women in the developing countries. This fact compelled the conference to secure the commitment of national commitments and multilateral agencies for greater allocation of resources to women. The women delegates brought it to the notice of world economists that the so called structural adjustment policies have left the bulk of the poor women high and dry with the benefits concerned by the privileged few. The equitable distribution of world's resources is a vital prerequisite to the real emancipation of women.

The first woman of USA, Ms. Hillary Clinton did strike a chord in the Beijing assembly with a remarkable assertion on the inalienable linkage between human rights and women's rights. She said that there is one message that echoes forth from this conference, it is that human rights are women's rights and women's rights are human rights. Equality without empowerment is a hollow concept. India has therefore taken an affirmative action that women get the position, resources and respect they deserve. As the head of the official delegation to the Beijing meet, Mr. Madhavrao Scindia, Union Minister for Human Resource Development (1995) said, that the government sees economic empowerment as important as poverty eradication and it has been our endeavour to encourage women to take control over their own finance. India also announced its decision to appoint a commission for women's rights to look into the human rights issues involving women.

Beijing Agenda

The platform for Action adopted the following measures to be taken at the UN, national and International level aimed at removing gender inequalities. The platform for Action covers 12 specific areas of concern. They are poverty, education, health, violence, arms conflicts, economic disparify, power-sharing institutions, human rights, mass-media, environment and the girl child.

Poverty

- To create social security systems wherever they do not exist
- To develop gender-sensitive national and international policies including those related to structural adjustment
- To provide poor women with economic opportunities and equal access to affordable housing, land, natural resources, credit and other services
- To devise statistical means to recognise and make visible the work including unpaid and domestic workers and their contribution to the national economics

Education

- To close the gender gap in primary and secondary school education by the year 2005
- To eradicate illiteracy of women worldwide by 2000 or another target date to be agreed at the conference
- To improve women's access to and provide funding for vocational training, science and technology
- To develop curricula, textbooks and teaching aids for free of gender stereotypes

Health

- To strengthen and re-orient health services in order to reduce maternal mortality
- To strengthen prevention programmes that address threats to women's health
- To make efforts to combat HIV/AIDS and other sexually transmitted diseases and recognise the impact of those diseases on women

- To promote research and increase funding for women's health issues and services

Violence

- To take integrated legal and social measures to prevent violence and protection of women
- To adopt measures to eliminate trafficking on women and eradicate violence against women who are vulnerable such as those with disabilities and migrant workers
- To study the cause of violence against women and initiate effective measures of prevention

Armed Conflicts

- To Increase and strengthen women's participation in conflict resolution
- To promote women's contribution to fostering a culture of peace
- To reduce the incidence of human rights abuses in conflict situations, protect refugee and displaced women and provide assistance to women of the colonies

Economic Disparity

- To enact laws to guarantee the rights of women and men to equal pay for equal work and adjust work patterns to promote the sharing of family responsibilities
- To provide women with equal access to resources like employment, markets and trade as well as information and technology
- To eliminate sexual harassment and other forms of discrimination in the workplace

Power-sharing

- To ensure women's full and equal participation in power structures and decision making

- To develop education and training to increase women's capacity to participate in decision-making and leadership
- To aim at gender balance in government bodies and the composition of delegation to the UN

Institutions

- To ensure that responsibility for the advancement of women is invested at the highest level of government
- To integrate gender perspective in all legislations, public policies, programmes and projects
- To collect and disseminate statistics showing gender impact of policies and programmes

Human Rights

- To encourage ratification of international human rights treaties and to promote their implementation
- To provide gender-sensitive human rights training to public officials
- To improve access to legal services and literacy through information campaigns and national training programmes

Mass Media

- To take steps to ensure women's access to information and the media on an equal basis
- To encourage elimination of gender stereotyping in the media through studies, campaigns and various forms of self-regulation by media organisations

Environment

- To involve women in environmental decision-making and integrate gender concerns in policies for sustainable development
- To assess the impact of development and environmental policies on women

Girl Child

- To eliminate all forms of discrimination as well negative cultural attitudes and practices against girl children
- To ensure that girl children should develop a positive self-image and have equal access to education and health care
- To project girl children from economic exploitation and eliminate violence against them

India in Search of Equality, Development and Peace

The International Women's Year coincided with the second wave of women's movement in India. Seventies witnessed increased number of women's organisations, mobilisations of women on specific issues and some steps taken up by the government. The period from Mexico to Beijing is important for women not only in India but all over the world. As pointed out by the country paper India (A Draft) for the World Conference on Women, Beijing 1995. From the Ultra Feminism of the sixties to the introspections on women's status in the seventies to women development in the eighties and to gender in the nineties has been a bumpy but short ride. From women's problems to women's issues finally to women's perspectives there has been a whole reshaping of paradigms of human development.

The appointment of the committee on the status of women in India by the Government in 1971 to undertake a Comprehensive examination or all the questions relating to the fight and status of women in the context of changing social and economic conditions in the country and new problems relating to the advancement of women was the first major attempt to comprehend women's status.

The Report of the Committee on the Status of Women Towards Equality submitted to government was an eye opener to the policymakers, social workers and academics. It pointed out that the dynamics of social change and development had affected the majority of women adversely and had created new imbalances and disparities. The Report stressed that any policy or movement for emancipation and development of women has to form a part of total movement for removal in inequalities and oppressive social institutions. After a debate on this Report, the parliament adopted a unanimous resolution urging the Prime Minister to initiate a comprehensive programme of legislative and administrative measures aimed to removing as far as possible the economic and social injustices, disabilities and discrimination to which Indian women continue to be subjected.

After the mandate from the parliament on the report of Committee on status of Women in India, the government framed a National plan of Action for women based on its suggestions and on the UN's world plan of Action. It was endorsed by National Committee under the chairmanship of the late Prime Minister Ms Indira Gandhi. It was appointed in 1976 to ensure a fair deal for women and as an alternative to the National commission recommended by the committee on status of Women in India and UN, world plan of Action. A women's Welfare and Development Bureau (WDB) was established in Ministry of social welfare to act as the nodal point with in the Government to co-ordinate polices and programmes and to initiate measures for women's development. It was backed by an inter-ministerial standing committee. Special cells for women were also established in the Ministries of Labour, Employment and Rural Development.

During 1978-79 as preparatory action for the Mid-Decade review, Government promoted conferences at state level which involved non-official organisations, researchers, women legislators and representatives of departments. These culminated in the National conference on women and Development sponsored by the Ministry of social welfare in Delhi in May 1979. In 1980 some national women's organisations and institutions specialising research on women submitted a memorandum to the Government entitled "Indian Women in the Eighties: Development Imperatives". After this, dialogue began between the Planning Commission, women's organisations, researchers and activists resulting in the inclusion of chapter on women and development in the sixth Five year Plan. Another important outcome of the consultations in the planning commission in 1980 was the involvement of the Council of Scientific and Industrial Research and Department of Science and Technology in Efforts to encourage women to science and technology.

In 1985, the Government of India established a separate department in the Ministry of Human Resource development for development of women and children. The department of women and child development acts as the machinery within Government to guide, co-ordinate and review the efforts of both governmental and non-governmental organisations working for the welfare and development of women and children. The Central Social Welfare Board which is an apex organization at the national level acts as an umbrella organisation networking through state welfare boards. Through them thousands of voluntary organizations are working for the welfare and development of women and children in the country. The National Institute of Public Co-operation and Child Development, (NIPCCD) New Delhi assists the Department in the areas of research and training relating to women and children. The Government of India has over twenty seven schemes for women. Some are women specific schemes and others are for both women and men. These schemes are located in different departments and ministries of the Government of India such as Rural Development, Labour, Education, Health, Science and Technology, Social Welfare, Women and Child Welfare Development, etc.

Since the declaration of International Women's Year (1975), new range of women's organisations have merged. Their activities ranging from health and education to protect against violence, rape and dowry. Women's movement, declaration of the International Women's Year and the decade have contributed to the change of governments approach to women's issues (The dynamics between women's groups and government bodies however are often complex and ambivalent). Today the state talks of empowerment of women as active agents participating in guiding their own development. While the International Women's Decade (1976-1985) was strong outside presence in managing the shift from welfare to development. The publication of the Report of the committee on the Status of Women in India (1974) was also very significant.

Reviewing the outcomes of the policy debates in its Report to the United Nations in 1985, the Government of India noted that major result was "a shift in cognition from viewing women as targets of welfare policies in the social sector to their emergence as critical groups of development". The country paper India (a draft) for the World Conference on Women, Beijing contains a chapter on "Report on India's response in the context of Nairobi Toward Looking Strategies". Some important policy initiatives are mentioned here. The Nation perspective plan for women up to 2000 AD (1988) is a set of recommendations aimed to women's welfare and development. Some of these recommendations are already implemented and some are under consideration. The Report of the National Commission for self-employed women and women in the informal sector. Shrama Shakti (1988) gives a realistic picture of the condition of women working in the informal sector made some useful recommendations. Setting up of the Rashtriya Mahila Kosh (RMK) National Credit Fund for Women by the Department of Women and Child Development in 1993 is a follow-up of one of its major recommendations. Another important policy initiatives are recommendations by the National Expert Committee on Women.

Prisoners (1986) and National Nutrition Policy (1993), 73rd and 74th Constitutional Amendments, acts of 1993 have brought the historic provision of reserving 30 per cent seats for women in all elected offices of local bodies. About one million women will enter public life through this. Under various poverty alleviation programmes of the rural development sector, 40 per cent of benefits have been reserved for women belonging to below poverty line groups i.e. whose annual income is below Rs.11000/- per annum.

There have been important programme interventions. During this period education, employment and awareness generation including legal literacy are major strategies for empowerment of women. The National Policy on Education (1986) lays stress on women's equality. The National Literacy Mission and the special focus on the girl-children have contributed to create a new climate. Some improvements in legislation pertaining to women's lives has taken place, especially on issues of rape, dowry and violence. There are schemes for welfare and support services for working women like hostels, day care centers, crèches, short-stay homes for girls and women, the Integrated Child Development Scheme and health care. A country-wide gender sensitisation programme has been launched in 1991-92 to bring change in societal attitude towards women.

The Eighth Five-year plan has adopted the strategy of employment and income generation for mainstreaming women into national development. Mahila Samriddhi Yojana (1993) to enable rural women to have control over their savings and financial resources in addition to National Credit Fund for women. There is also a special programme launched for school drop-out adolescent girls (1990) for betterment of their lives. The Integrated Child Development Service (ICDS) presently world's largest Primary Health Care System, family planning package with maternal and child health facilities have brought some positive change in women's health status. To check the increasing unemployment rate of women some steps were taken like reserving certain percentage for women in employment linked programmes like Integrated Rural Development Programme (IRDP), Jawahar Rozgar Yojana (JRY), Development of Women and Children in Rural Areas (DWCRA) and Support to Training and Employment Programme (STEP). Some conscious efforts were made to give visibility to women's work in 1991 census. According to the 1991 census the work participation rate of females rose from 14.22 per cent in 1971 to 19.67 per cent in 1981 and to 22.27 per cent in 1991.

The government has taken specific measures for institutional support. The National Commission for Women (1992) is setup to study and monitor all matters relating to the constitutional and legal safeguards provided for women and to review existing legislations and suggest amendments and look into complaints regarding deprivation of women's rights. State commissions are also set up on similar lines.

The historical, economic and socio-cultural forces have given rise to existing disparities. Women are often perceived as targets of welfare policies and not as critical groups for development. It is common experience that special mechanism and machineries set up to advance the cause of women, very often have the opposite result by treating women as a "Special Category" i.e. by marginalising them.

Bibliography

1. Agnew Vijay (1979), *Elite Women in Indian Politics*, Vikas Publishing House, New Delhi.
2. Ajeet and Arpana Cour (1976), *Directory of Indian Women Today*, India International Publications, New Delhi.
3. Altekar A.S (1978), *The Position of Women in Hindu Civilization*, Motilal Banarsidas, Delhi.
4. Andersen L. (1983) Margeret, *Thinking About Women*, Macmillan Publishers, USA.
5. Anjana Matra Sinha (1993), *Women in a Changing Society*, Ashish Publishing House, New Delhi.
6. Annie Parti, Asha Hans (2003), *Women, Disability and Identity*, Sage Publications, New Dehi.
7. Aparna Basu (1976), *The Role of Women in the Indian Struggle for Freedom: From Purdah to Modernity*, Vikas Publishing House, New Delhi.
8. Aravind Kumar (1999), *Human Rights and Social Movement*, Anmol Publications, New Delhi.
9. Barbara Ryan (1992), *Feminism and the Women's Movements*, Routledge, New York.

10. Baig Tara Ali (1958), *Women of India*, Publications Division, Government of India, New Delhi.

11. Baig Tara Ali (1976), *India's Women Power*, S. Chand and Co. (P) Ltd., New Delhi.

12. Bakshi S.R (1987), *Gandhi and Status of Women*, Criterion Publications, New Delhi.

13. Bhargava B.S. and Vidya K.C (1992), *Position of Women in Political Institutions*, Journal of Rural Development, Vol II, No. 5 September, 1992.

14. Bipin Chandra (1972), *Freedom Struggle*, National Book Trust, New Delhi.

15. Chaudhary J.B (1956), *Women in Vedic Rituals*, Pracyavani Publications, Calcutta.

16. Chattopadhyaya Kamaladevi (1982), *Indian Women: Battle for Freedom*, Abhinav Publications, New Delhi.

17. Chapman, Jane Roberts (1976), *Economic Independence for Women: The Foundation for Equal Rights*, Vol. I, Sage Publications, New Delhi.

18. Cormack .M (1961), *The Hindu Women*, Asia Publishing House, Bombay.

19. Daran D.V (1981), *Hinduism at a Glance*, United Printers Syndicate, Madras.

20. Dayaram Gidumal (1989), *Status of Women in India*, Star Publications, New Delhi.

21. De Souza, Alfred (1975), *Women in Contemporary India*, Manohar Publications, New Delhi.

22. De Souza, Alfred (1980), *Women in Contemporary India and South Asia*, Manohar Publications, New Delhi.

23. Devaki Jain (1975), *Indian Women*, Ministry of Information and Broadcasting, New Delhi.

24. Desai Neera (1957), *Women in Modern India*, Vora & Co. Publishers, Bombay.

25. Desai Neera and Vibhuti Patel (1985), *Indian Women, Change and Challenge in the International Decade 1975-1985*, Popular Prakashan, Bombay.

26. Desai Neera and Krishnaraj Maitreyi (1987), *Women and Society in India*, Ajanta Publications, New Delhi.

27. Digumarti Bhaskar Rao, Digumarti Pushpalatha Rao (1999), *Status of World's Women*, Discovery Publishing House, New Delhi.

28. Dubois J.A Abbe (1973), *Hindu Manners, Customs and Ceremonies*, Mamata Publications, New Delhi.

29. Dutt M.N (1937), *Status of Women*, Mahendra Publishing Committee, Calcutta.

30. Gandhi M.K (1919), *Women of Modern India*, Bombay.

31. Ganguli B.N, Emma Goldman (1979), *Potrait of a Rebel Woman*, Allied Publishers, New Delhi.

32. Ghadially Rehana (1988), *Women in Indian Society*, Sage Publications, New Delhi.

33. Ghosh S.K (1989), *Indian Women Through the Ages*, Ashish Publishing House, New Delhi.

34. Ghosh S.K (1981), *Women in Policing,* Light and Life Publications, Delhi.

35. Gupta A.R (1982), *Women in Hindu Society*, Jyotsna Prakashan, New Delhi.

36. Haralambos M. and R.M. Heald (1980), *Sociology—Themes and Perspectives*, Oxford University Press, Delhi.

37. Hansa Mehta (1919), *Indian Women and Gandhiji*, Butala & Company, Delhi.

38. Hate C.A (1969), *Changing Status of Women*, Allied Publishers, Bombay.

39. Hazel D'Lima (1983), *Women in Local Government*, Concept Publishing Company, New Delhi.

40. Huber, Joan (1973), *Changing Women and Changing Society*, The University of Chicago.

41. Immanuel (1969), *Women and Development*, Karnavati Publication, Gujarat.

42. Indira Devi M. (1994), *Women and Indian Nationalism*, Vikas Publishing House, New Delhi.

43. Indira (1955), *The Status of Women in Ancient India*, Motilal Banarasidas, Banaras.

44. Inderjeet Kaur (1983), *Status of Hindu Women in India*, Chugh Publications, Allahabad.

45. Janaki K. (1999), *Role of Women in Freedom Struggle* in Andhra Pradesh, Neelkamal Publications, Hyderabad.

46. Jain Devaki (1980), *Women's Quest for Power*, Vikas Publishing House, New Delhi.

47. Jain Devaki (1975), *Indian Women*, Allied Publishers, New Delhi.

48. Jessie B. Tellis Nayak (1983), *Indian Womenhood Then and Now*, Satya Prakashan Sanchar Kendra, Indore.

49. Jogesa Chandra Ghosa (1982), *Hindu Women of India*, Bimla Publishing House, New Delhi.

50. Jyothi Mitra (1997), *Women and Society—Equality and Empowerment*, Kanishka Publishers, New Delhi.

51. Jyotsna Chatterji (1900), *Religions and the Status of Women*, Uppal Publishing House, New Delhi.

52. Kaur Manmohan (1958), *Role of Women in Freedom Movement in India* 1857-1947, Sterling Publications, Jallundar.

53. Kaushik Susheela (1984), *Women's Oppression: Patterns and Perspectives*, Ajanta Publications, Delhi.

54. Kapadia K.M (1966), *Marriage and Family in India*, Oxford University Press, Bombay.

55. Kane P.V (1941), *History of Dharmashastra*, Bhandakar Oriental Research Institute, Poona.

56. Kapur Promilla (1970), *Changing Status of Working Women in India*, Vikas Publishing House, New Delhi.

57. Kapur Promilla (1970), *Marriage and the Working Women in India*, Vikas Publishing House, New Delhi.

58. Kidwai, Sheikh M.H (1978), *Women Under Different Social and Religious Laws*, Light and Life Publishers, New Delhi.

59. Krishna Murthy (1989), *Women in Colonial India*, Oxford University Press, New Delhi.

60. Kumar A. (2006), *Women's Movement*, Anmol Publications, New Delhi.

61. Kumar Ashok (1989), *Indian Women Towards 21st Century*, Criterion Publications, New Dehi.

62. Lalitha Devi U. (1982), *Status and Employment of Women in India*, B.R. Publishing Corporation, New Delhi.

63. Leela Kasturi and Veena Mazumbar (1994), *Women and Indian Nationalism*, Vikas Publishing House, New Delhi.

64. Lila Samatani (1968), *Status of Women in Vedic Times*, Maharshi Academy of Vedic Sciences, Ahmedabad.

65. Madhu Shastri (1990), *Status of Hindu Women*, RBSA Publications, Delhi.

66. Maurya S.D (1988), *Women in India*, Chugh Publications, Allahabad.

67. Malladi Subbamma (1994), *Women's Movements and Associations*, Mahilabhyudaya Samstha, Hyderabad.

68. Malladi Subbamma (1994), *Women and Social Reform*, Book Links Corporation, Hyderabad.

69. Manmohan Kaur (1962), *Women in India's Freedom Struggle*, Sterling Publishers, Delhi.

70. Malladi Subbamma (1994), *Status of Indian Women*, Malladi Subbamma Trust, Hyderabad.

71. Malladi Subbamma (1994), *Women in Changing Society*, Malladi Subbamma Trust, Hyderabad.

72. Mate C.A (1973), *Changing Status of Women in Post-Independence India*, Allied Publishers, Bombay.

73. Manohar K.M (1983), *Socio-economic Status of Indian Women*, Seema Publications, Delhi.

74. Mahajan V.S (1993), *Women's Contribution to India's Economic and Social Development*, Deep and Deep Publications, New Delhi.

75. Mehta, Sushila (1982), *Revolution and Status of Women in India*, Metropolitan, New Delhi.

76. Menan, Lakshmi (1980), *Political Rights of Women in India*, Asian Publishing House, Bombay.

77. Mishra R.C (2006), *Women in India: Towards Gender Equality*, Authors Press, New Delhi.

78. Nanda B.R (1976), *Indian Women from Purdah to Modernity*, Vikas Publishing House, Delhi.

79. Neera Desai and Maitreyi Krishnaraj (1990), *Women and Society in India*, Ajantha Publications, Delhi.

80. Niroj Sinha (2000), *Women in Indian Politics*, Gyan Publishing House, New Delhi.

81. Pandya B.A (1994), *Women Organisations and Development*, Illustrated Book Publishers, Jaipur.

82. Paul Chowdhary (1992), *Women, Welfare and Development*, Inter India Publications, New Delhi.

83. Pratima Asthana (1974), *Women's Movement in India*, Vikas Publishing House, Delhi.

84. Pratibha Jain, Rajan Mahajan (1996), *Women Images*, Rawat Publications, Jaipur.

85. Promila Kapur (1970), *Marriage and the Working Women in India*, Vikas Publications, New Delhi.

86. Raj Pruthi, Bela Rani Sharma (1995), *Social Movements and Women*, Anmol Publications, New Delhi.

87. Rajkumari Amrit Kaur (1973), *Gandhi and Women*, Viswabharathi Publishing House, Delhi.

88. Ram S. (2004), *Women Through Ages*, Commonwealth Publishers, New Delhi.

89. Rehana Ghadially (1988), *Women in Indian Society*, Sage Publications, New Delhi.

90. Reddy P.R. Sumangala (1998), *Women in Development, Perspective from Selected States of India*, Vol II, B.R.Publications, New Delhi.

91. Sarada Rath, Navaneeta Rath (2001), *Women in India: A Search for Identity*, Anmol Publications, New Delhi.

92. Sangeetha Mishra (1993), *Status of Women in Changing Urban Hindu Family*, Radha Publications, New Delhi.

93. Shakuntala Jayal (1966), *The Status of Women in the Epics*, Motilal Banarasidas, Patna.

94. Sushila Agarwal (1988), *Status of Women*, Printwell Publishers, Jaipur.

95. Sharan B.R (1992), *Status of Indian Women: a Historical Perspective*, Uppal Publishing House, New Delhi.

96. Shah Kalpana (1984), *Women's Liberation and Voluntary Action*, Ajanta Publications, Delhi.

97. Suguna B. (1994), *Working Women and Religion*, Discovery Publishing House, New Delhi.

98. Suguna B. (2006), *Empowerment of Rural Women Through Self Help Groups*, Discovery Publishing House, New Delhi.

99. Sudha Rani Shrivastava (1999), *Women in India*, Commonwealth Publishers, New Delhi.

100. Sudha Gogate (1988), *Status of Women*, Shubhada Saraswat Prakashan, Pune.

101. Srinivas M.N (1978), *The Changing Position of Indian Women*, Oxford University Press, New Delhi.

102. Suseela Subramanyam, Meera Chakravorthy (2005), *Women in Nation Building*, A Southern Economist Publication, Bangalore.

103. Sushila Mehta (1982), *Revolution and Status of Women in India*, Metropolitan Book & Co., New Delhi.

104. Tandon R.K (1999), *Status of Women in Contemporary World*, Commonwealth Publishers, New Delhi.

105. Thomas R. (1964), *Indian Women Through the Ages*, Asia Publishing House, Bombay.

106. Upadhya Bhagwat Saran (1974), *Women in Rigveda*, Schand and Co, New Delhi.

107. Urmila Phadnis and Indira Malani (1928), *Women of the World Illusion and Reality*, Vikas Publishing House, New Delhi.

108. Umashankar Jha, Arti Mehta, Latika Menon (1998), *Status of Indian Women: Crisis and Conflict in Gender Issues* (Vol 2), Kanishka Publishers, New Delhi.

109. Usharao N.J (1985), *Women in Developing Society*, Ashish Publishing House, New Delhi.

110. Vaikuntham (1982), *Education and Social Change in South India: Andhra, 1880-1920*, New Era Publications, Madras.

111. Verma S.P (2005), *Status of Women in Modern India*, Deep and Deep Publications, New Delhi.

112. Vijay Kaushik (1997), *Women's Movements and Human Rights*, Pointer Publishers, Jaipur.

Index

❑❑❑